Strive to Finish First

What Can African Americans Learn from Nigerian Immigrants?

By Janssen Brooks

Copyright © 2023

Naija, land of hope, where dreams dey take flight,

We dey grind, we dey hustle, from morning till night.

"Naija No Dey Carry Last*,"* na our battle cry,

With passion and power, we aim for the sky.

About the Author

Born in Aliceville, Alabama, both of Janssen Brook's parents were educators.

He is the youngest of seven children. He attended the public schools in his hometown. He graduated from Alabama A&M University with a B.S. Degree in Social Planning and a M.S. Degree in Urban Studies. He has worked as a City Planner and a Civil Defense planner. He has worked for many years in the sales profession. Janssen is currently the owner of Envision Financial Strategies LLC, a Financial Services firm that helps clients with Life Insurance, long-term care Planning, and Retirement Income Planning.

For two and a half years, Janssen hosted a live blog radio show called The Council of Elders Call-In Talk Show. The show focused on bridging the gap between youth and elders. Some of the topics of conversation were How to bridge the academic achievement gap between Blacks and Whites in the U.S. The idea for this book came when a guest on the show mentioned the success of Nigerians in the U.S.

Acknowledgment

I wrote this book because I wanted to share what I thought was wonderful, inspirational, and positive news.

When I first learned how well Nigerians were thriving in the United States, it was a surprise to me; I was inspired. I then researched online and found out that it was true. I mentioned this news to many of my friends and family, and they, too, were surprised. I told myself that more people should know about this because this is very inspirational news.

During this process, I had a chance to talk with many Nigerian Americans who shared with me some concepts and principles that were impressive. Many of these ideas I have shared in this book.

I believe that one way to improve one's life is to model someone's mindset and behavior. Especially as long as they are honest and ethical. One can glean ideas and information that can change his or her life for the better.

In life, no one path is right for everybody. I hope something in this book helps someone along the way in their life.

There is so much more information that could have been added to this little book. However, you can do further research because much more study should be done on this subject to improve the lives of more people. I want to thank my wife Cheryl, who encouraged me throughout this process, and my daughter Eliza, who makes me the proud father of a wonderful young lady.

I want to thank the many Nigerian Americans who gave me insights into some of their core values and philosophies. I want to thank my publishers, Logo Cosmic, for their professionalism and guidance throughout this project. Most of all, I want to thank you, the reader, for picking up this book. I hope that something in it will help you to succeed in reaching your dreams and goals.

Table of Contents

Prologue

Book Prologue Outline:

Greetings, my name is Janssen Brooks. I was born and raised in the deep southern State of Alabama in 1953, a mere eighty-eight years after the United States abolished slavery. Our town, Aliceville, was steeped in the lingering echoes of this tumultuous history and the enduring struggle for racial equality. The impacts of this turbulent past were inescapable; they shaped my life and influenced the fabric of my identity as an African-American man.

Growing up in the United States, especially the Deep South, in the post-slavery era, I was surrounded by stories of resistance, survival, and courage from the African-American community. Yet, it wasn't until I came across a startling fact that my curiosity took a new turn.

Despite the socioeconomic barriers that exist for immigrants, Nigerians had not only managed to establish themselves in America but were thriving in unprecedented ways. I was astounded. They were reported to be the most successful immigrant group in America - a feat that didn't come without its set of challenges.

The success of Nigerian immigrants seemed like an anomaly in an environment where immigrant communities, particularly those of color, often faced systemic disadvantages. I found myself pondering, "How did they do it?" What unique traits or cultural elements enabled them to navigate the challenges of immigration and achieve such remarkable success? Was there a special recipe? And if so, could it be replicated? These questions compelled me to delve deeper into the phenomenon of Nigerian success in America. As I continue this exploration, I hope to unravel the remarkable journey of these resilient individuals and, along the way, offer valuable lessons for our African-American community and beyond.

Before we embark on this journey of discovery, it's essential to pause and honor the brave African-American leaders and everyday heroes who paved the way for progress. It was their unyielding perseverance and immense courage that catalyzed social change, provided the tools for upward mobility, and planted the seeds of opportunity that immigrants of color can now sow.

From the heroic figures like Sojourner Truth, who fought for both women's and Black people's rights, to the profound influence of Martin Luther King Jr., who's famous "I Have a Dream" speech echoes the cry for equality even today. The charismatic Malcolm X, who advocated for Black empowerment and self-identification, and Rosa Parks, whose singular act of defiance sparked the Montgomery Bus Boycott, gave impetus to the Civil Rights Movement. These, along with countless other known and unsung heroes, have been pivotal in the struggle for equality since 1865.

Yet, it wasn't just the leaders who forged this path. Every African-American man, woman, and child who endured, resisted, and persisted in the face of brutal adversity has been an integral part of this struggle. Each one contributed to shaping a society where opportunities for success have expanded and immigrants of color, like the Nigerians, can come, thrive, and claim their version of the American Dream.

Their collective sacrifice laid the groundwork for the freedoms and opportunities that we, as a community, enjoy today. The progress they engendered is the foundation upon which immigrant success stories have been built. It is, therefore, essential to remember and honor their struggles as we celebrate the achievements of those who have benefited from their courageous endeavors. This homage is a small token of our profound gratitude and a reminder of our roots and the strength of our community.

Reflecting upon the African-American community, I have observed a shift in mindset that is disconcerting. Once upon a time, our community held a potent sense of strength and capability. Despite the harsh realities of racism and discrimination, our forebears rose above these challenges with unwavering resilience and a deep-rooted belief in their intelligence, strength, and capacity for greatness. Today, I fear we have strayed from this empowering mindset. There seems to be an air of diminished self-belief, a more submissive acceptance of the societal constraints that hold us back. This departure from our legacy of strength saddens me. I yearn for the revitalization of our original mindset, a reconnection with our potent past, and the reclaiming of our collective power.

My research revealed Nigerians to be the most successful immigrant group in the nation. Despite the myriad of challenges associated with immigration, they have not merely survived but thrived, often reaching the zenith in their respective fields. This realization filled me with admiration for their tenacity and accomplishment.

The remarkable success of second-generation Nigerians in the United States poses a compelling question: What unique mindset and cultural values have propelled Nigerian immigrants and their descendants to such notable heights? This exploration is not just about unraveling the secrets behind their achievements but also about understanding a community's unwavering commitment to progress and excellence.

At the heart of the Nigerian immigrant experience is a profound ethos centered around hard work, education, and an unwavering faith in progress. This mindset is not born out of a desire for mere survival or the pursuit of material wealth alone; it is a deeply ingrained belief in the transformative power of education and the relentless pursuit of excellence. Nigerian immigrants often arrive in America with a clear purpose: to create a better future for themselves and their families. This purpose is not fueled by a quest for handouts but by a steadfast determination to work hard and seize opportunities.

Education is revered within the Nigerian community as a fundamental pillar for success. It is viewed not just as a pathway to a career but as a vital tool for personal and communal upliftment. This reverence for education is passed down through generations, becoming a core component of the Nigerian identity in America. The impressive representation of Nigerians in prestigious institutions like Harvard and Yale is a testament to this cultural emphasis. It's not just about getting an education; it's about excelling in it.

Nigerians in America, particularly in the field of medicine, are not just participating; they are leading and setting new standards. This overachievement is a reflection of a broader trend within the community, where Nigerian families consistently outperform the average American in terms of income and educational attainment. This overachievement is a direct result of the disciplined, goal-oriented upbringing that Nigerian children receive.

The Nigerian parenting style is often characterized by discipline and high expectations. Parents instill in their children the values of hard work and perseverance, teaching them that success is earned, not given. This disciplined approach extends beyond academics, influencing attitudes towards sports and other extracurricular activities. The focus is always on maintaining a balance, with education remaining the priority.

A distinctive feature of the Nigerian immigrant narrative is the remarkable progress observed from one generation to the next. The first generation, often the immigrant parents, lays a solid foundation through sacrifice and hard work. They are deeply involved in their children's lives, often making significant personal and financial sacrifices to ensure their children have access to quality education and opportunities. This involvement is not merely transactional; it's a profound commitment to their children's future.

The Nigerian approach to success is holistic. It's not just about academic achievement; it's about developing a well-rounded individual. Parents dont push kids into sports but if they are engaged athletics activities, it is always with the caveat that education should not be compromised.

The Nigerian immigrant community in America is characterized by strong support systems. Families and community groups often come together to provide support, share resources, and celebrate achievements. This sense of community plays a crucial role in the success of Nigerian immigrants, providing a network of encouragement and assistance.

As we observe the progress of Nigerian families in America, there is a growing anticipation of what the future holds, especially for the third and subsequent generations. These generations are expected to surpass the achievements of their predecessors, fueled by the values, discipline, and educational foundations laid by the first and second generations. They inherit not only the aspirations of their forebears but also the cultural and intellectual capital that comes with a deep-rooted emphasis on education and excellence.

The story of high-achieving second-generation Nigerians in America is one of resilience, hard work, and a relentless pursuit of excellence. It is a narrative that highlights the power of a collective mindset geared towards progress, the transformative role of education, and the enduring impact of cultural values and parental involvement. As we delve further into this remarkable journey, we uncover not just the secrets of a community's success but also the universal lessons that can inspire and guide us all.

The essence of this book revolves around inspiration, empowerment, and transformation. As we explore the fascinating success story of Nigerian immigrants in America, we do not merely celebrate their achievements; we extract, understand, and emphasize the ethics, principles, and mindsets that fueled their journey.

These range from a high regard for education, unwavering perseverance, and inherent resilience to high expectations for personal achievement. By unpacking these core aspects, this book aims to provide a reference point, a source of inspiration for African Americans to reinvigorate their ethos and revive their innate capacities.

However, the purpose of this book is not to create a definitive guide to success or to advocate for a homogenized path to prosperity. Instead, it is to underscore that we have, within us, the potential for greatness, the capacity to overcome, and the strength to excel. It's about re-establishing a sense of self-belief, reinforcing the tenacity that has been a part of our narrative for centuries, and encouraging each individual to harness their unique abilities.

The success story of Nigerian immigrants is presented as an inspiring example of what can be achieved with the right mindset and ethics.

The hope is that this examination will ignite a spark within African Americans, reminding them of their potential and inspiring them to nurture these successful characteristics and make their unique imprint on the tapestry of American success stories.

Chapter 1 – The Beginning

Introduction

Nigerians have etched a distinct path in the world diaspora, especially within the United States. They have carved out a unique niche in this multicultural melting pot, proudly taking their place as the most educated immigrant group. An impressive percentage of Nigerians are college graduates, surpassing all other ethnicities and immigrant groups. Furthermore, they're predominant in white-collar professions and have income levels significantly higher than many of their counterparts. This pattern of achievement and upward mobility is fascinating, leading to numerous studies aiming to unravel the contributing factors to this exceptional success story.

In this comprehensive exploration, we will dive deep into the rich tapestry of Nigerian immigration to the United States, mapping their journey from the shores of Africa to the land of opportunities. We will present a vast array of statistics highlighting the strength of the Nigerian diaspora in the context of their educational accomplishments, employment status, and income brackets. Following that, we will meticulously uncover the intrinsic attributes and external factors that amplify the success of Nigerian immigrants, offering an insightful examination of their journey.

Nigerians don't just inhabit a place in American society; they have fundamentally enriched it. The story of their journey, their struggles, and their victories is a testament to the strength of the human spirit and the power of dreams. This remarkable community has not only thrived but also made significant contributions to the economic, social, and cultural fabric of the United States.

The trends that underscore their success are certainly not random. Nigerians' soaring educational achievements are a reflection of a deeply ingrained cultural belief in the transformative power of knowledge. Their representation in white-collar jobs isn't merely an indicator of their professional aspirations but also an affirmation of their determination to excel and their relentless pursuit of excellence.

Yet, their accomplishments are not just a matter of statistics and percentages. They are the stories of countless individuals who dared to dream, to cross oceans, to build a new life in a foreign land, and to create a better future for themselves and their children. Their tale of tenacity and triumph is both inspiring and instructive, reflecting the potential inherent in each immigrant story.

By delving into the history of Nigerian immigration to the United States, we not only chart the path they have trodden but also illuminate the way forward for other immigrants. This journey, often punctuated by adversity and propelled by aspiration, offers valuable insights into the immigrant experience.

By highlighting the statistical representation of the Nigerian diaspora, we present an objective assessment of their position within American society. The figures tell an eloquent story of triumph over adversity, of aspirations realized, and of dreams nurtured into reality. These statistics do not just quantify the Nigerian immigrant's success; they testify to their Capacity to transform challenges into opportunities for growth opportunities and to navigate the complex landscape of a new culture, society, and economy.

Finally, the exploration of the key attributes that bolster Nigerian immigrants' success provides a roadmap for others. This is not merely a record of the Nigerian success story but also a guidebook that highlights the values, attitudes, and strategies that can enable others to emulate their achievements.

In a world increasingly defined by global migration, the success of Nigerian immigrants offers a beacon of hope. It demonstrates the potential of immigrants to enhance their adopted homes, contributing richly to the cultural, social, and economic landscape. By delving into the intricacies of their journey, we don't just celebrate their victories; we also understand the lessons they offer and the path they have paved for the journeys yet to come. This is not just a Nigerian story; it is an

American story, an immigrant story, and a global story. It is a story of the human spirit's resilience, aspiration, and indefatigable quest for a better life.

History of Nigerian Immigration to the United States In the grand tapestry of global migration, the journey of Nigerians to the United States tells a stirring tale of resilience, ambition, and overcoming the shadows of a challenging past.

The Nigerian-American diaspora stands today as a vibrant testament to the transformative power of opportunity, education, and unwavering determination.

Post-Civil War Migration to the U.S

The early seeds of this journey were sown in the initial wave of Nigerian immigration in the early 20th century, largely composed of students and professionals drawn to the United States by the Lure of educational and professional growth opportunities. This migration, happening in the aftermath of the transatlantic slave trade, opened a new chapter for Nigerians in the Land of Opportunity.

The second wave, which started post-1960, was triggered by Nigeria's independence from British colonial rule. This period saw a more diverse and substantial influx of Nigerian immigrants from varied socioeconomic backgrounds. This generation of immigrants carried with them not only the dreams of prosperity but also the collective will to overcome the lingering scars of colonial rule and slavery.

In the 1980s, the third and most substantial wave of Nigerian immigration began, fueled by various factors. Nigeria faced an economic downturn and political instability at home, while the United States opened its arms wider to immigrants from all corners of the globe with the landmark Immigration and Nationality Act of 1965. This act, abolishing national-origin quotas, beckoned Nigerians from all walks of life.

This era also brought to the fore a conscious move to shake off the stigmatizing stereotypes and post-colonial mindsets. Drawing strength from their rich cultural heritage and emboldened by their aspirations, Nigerian immigrants challenged and overcame the racial biases and discrimination rooted in a history marred by slavery. They redefined their identity in this new homeland, rewriting the narrative from victims of historical injustices to active contributors in their adopted society.

Today, the United States is home to approximately 350,000 Nigerian immigrants, contributing significantly to the vibrant multicultural ethos of the country. The largest communities reside in New York City, Houston, and Washington, D.C., infusing these cities with their rich traditions, culture, and intellectual capital.

These Nigerians have not only made the United States their home but also thrived here. They have confronted and overcome the debilitating legacy of slavery and colonialism through a potent blend of education, hard work, and cultural pride. It's a story of transformation, from shackles to scholarships, from chains to Chairs of professional and academic establishments, from oppression to inclusive leadership and equality opportunities.

In the heart of this extraordinary journey lies a valuable lesson for all: that history, no matter how dark, need not bind us, that the spirit of humanity, fueled by education and opportunity, can overcome even the deepest of scars, and that our past, however painful, can be a stepping stone, not a stumbling block, on the road to progress. As we navigate the complexities of our diverse, interconnected world, the story of Nigerian immigrants in the United States serves as a powerful beacon of hope, resilience, and possibility.

Statistics on Nigerian Immigrants in the United States

Educational Attainment

Nigerian immigrants are the most educated immigrant group in the United States. In 2018, 60% of Nigerian immigrants aged 25 and older had a bachelor's degree or higher, compared to 33% of all immigrants and 30% of the native-born population. The percentage of Nigerian immigrants with a bachelor's degree has been increasing over time. In 1980, only 30% of Nigerian immigrants had a bachelor's degree. This number has increased by 30% over the past 40 years.

The high educational attainment of Nigerian immigrants is due to a number of factors. These factors include:

I. The strong emphasis on education in Nigerian culture. Education is highly valued in Nigerian culture, and parents often invest heavily in their children's education.

II. The availability of scholarships and other financial aid for Nigerian students. The Nigerian government and private organizations offer a number of scholarships and other financial aid to Nigerian students who want to study abroad.

III. The high quality of education in Nigeria. Nigerian universities are some of the best in Africa, and they offer a wide range of courses in a variety of disciplines.

Employment

Nigerian immigrants are more likely to be employed in white-collar occupations than other immigrant groups. In 2018, 60% of Nigerian immigrants were employed in management, professional, and related occupations, compared to 45% of all immigrants and 37% of the native-born population.

The most common occupations for Nigerian immigrants are:

I. Computer and mathematical occupations
II. Business and financial occupations
III. Healthcare practitioners and technical occupations.

Engineering Occupations

Legal occupations

Nigerian immigrants are also more likely to be self-employed than other immigrant groups. In 2018, 14% of Nigerian immigrants were self-employed, compared to 10% of all immigrants and 8 % of the native-born population.

Income

Nigerian immigrants have higher incomes than other immigrant groups. In 2018, the median household income for Nigerian immigrants was $77,000, compared to $59,000 for all immigrants and $61,000 for the native-born population.

The income gap between Nigerian immigrants and other immigrant groups has been increasing over time. In 1980, the median household income for Nigerian immigrants was only slightly higher than the median household income for all immigrants. However, the income gap has widened since then, and Nigerian immigrants now have significantly higher incomes than other immigrant groups.

There are a number of factors that contribute to the high incomes of Nigerian immigrants. These factors include:

I. The high educational attainment of Nigerian immigrants. As discussed above, Nigerian immigrants are more likely to have a college degree than other immigrant groups. This gives them a competitive edge in the job market and leads to higher salaries.

II. The high employment rate of Nigerian immigrants. As discussed above, Nigerian immigrants are more likely to be employed than other immigrant groups. This also contributes to their higher incomes.

III. The high occupational status of Nigerian immigrants. As discussed above,

Nigerian immigrants are more likely to be employed in white-collar occupations than other immigrant groups. These occupations typically pay higher salaries.

Factors that Contribute to the Success of Nigerian Immigrants

The success story of Nigerian immigrants in the United States is a multi-faceted tale that is deeply rooted in social, economic, and cultural factors. A multitude of overlapping variables shape their experiences, making the journey of each individual a unique one. Let's delve into these factors, supported by data and insights from social sciences, that underpin their remarkable accomplishments.

High educational attainment: A hallmark of the Nigerian diaspora is their high level of education. A research report by the Migration Policy Institute states that Nigerian immigrants are often armed with academic degrees upon their arrival or rigorously pursued after settling in the United States. With 61% of Nigerian immigrants aged 25 and older possessing at least a bachelor's degree, as per the 2018 American Community Survey data, their educational attainment outshines the overall U.S. population. This competitive edge significantly increases their chances of securing well-paying jobs and accelerating their socioeconomic advancement.

I. **Strong work ethic:** The indomitable Nigerian work ethic is another crucial factor. Nigerian culture's emphasis on diligence and Tenacity, as suggested by studies in ethnopsychology, endows Nigerian immigrants with a tireless commitment to work. This tenacity finds its roots in the Igbo and Yoruba cultures, the two largest ethnic groups in Nigeria, both of which emphasize the virtues of hard work and personal achievement.

II. **Family support:** The importance of familial support cannot be understated. As suggested by a study published in the Journal of Comparative Family Studies, the Nigerian family unit is characterized by collective responsibility and mutual support, often transcending nuclear family boundaries to include extended kin. This close-knit support network provides not only emotional stability but also financial assistance and practical help, laying a solid foundation for their success in the United States.

III. **Cultural values:** A distinctive characteristic of Nigerian society is its high regard for education, hard work, and familial ties. Research in the field of cultural anthropology suggests that these values, firmly ingrained in the Nigerian mindset, have been instrumental in guiding their path to success. This deep-rooted cultural orientation, where success is synonymous with academic and professional achievement, often acts as a motivating force driving their journey in the United States.

IV. **Social networks:** Finally, social networks play a crucial role in the success of Nigerian immigrants. As noted by sociologists studying immigrant integration, establishing strong social ties within their community provides a support system that aids in overcoming initial resettlement challenges. These networks, comprising fellow immigrants, provide valuable information, job leads, and emotional support, thus amplifying their opportunities for success.

In essence, the success of Nigerian immigrants in the United States is a testament to their indomitable spirit, tenacity, and unwavering commitment to education and work, undergirded by robust familial support and cultural values. At the same time, it's worth noting that their accomplishments underscore the vital role supportive social networks play in immigrant communities, reminding us that success is seldom a solitary journey but a communal effort. This nuanced understanding of the Nigerian diaspora's accomplishments offers us profound insights into how the interplay of individual, cultural, and social factors shape immigrant success, contributing to the rich tapestry of the American immigrant experience.

Chapter 2 - Nigerian Ancestry and the Atlantic Slave Trade

The narrative of the United States is deeply intertwined with the histories and struggles of various groups, one of which is the people of Nigerian ancestry. The first recorded presence of these individuals on American soil can be traced back to the early days of the Atlantic slave trade. Unlike other immigrants who journeyed in search of better prospects, the Nigerian ancestors arrived on the shores of the New World not out of choice, but due to a heinous system of human trafficking. This introduction will delve into the origins of these early Nigerian arrivals, the major African export points they were shipped from, and their primary destinations in the Americas.

Major Export Points in Africa: Gateways of Despair

On the vast African continent, two ports, in particular, stood out during the 17th and 18th centuries as epicenters of the Atlantic slave trade: Calabar and Badagry, specifically Gberefu Island. These ports were not merely transit points; they were the final African soil many enslaved individuals would touch before facing the treacherous journey across the Atlantic. It is poignant to imagine the multitudes of Nigerians, hailing from diverse tribes and regions, amassed in these ports – their destinies altered forever.

The involvement of English ships in these ports was more than just significant; it was predominant. These vessels, funded and sanctioned by powerful English merchants and aristocrats, would anchor off the coasts of Calabar and Badagry, waiting to be loaded with 'cargo'. This 'cargo' was, in reality, human beings – men, women, and children – ripped from their homes and families, destined for lifetimes of servitude in a foreign land. The magnitude of the English involvement in this trade underscores the vast economic interests intertwined with this inhumane business.

Destination Points in America: New Lands, Unfamiliar Horizons

Upon surviving the perilous journey known infamously as the 'Middle Passage', these enslaved Africans would find themselves in various parts of the Americas. However, there was a discernible pattern to their destinations, especially for those hailing from the Bight of Biafra and, more specifically, the Igbo hinterland. The state of Virginia, with its burgeoning plantations and insatiable demand for labor, emerged as a primary destination. It became the new, forced home for thousands of Igbo and other Biafran natives.

Yet, Virginia was not the sole receiver of these enslaved individuals. Maryland, another state with deep agricultural roots, was also a primary destination. The state's tobacco farms and other agricultural enterprises ensured a constant demand for labor, and this demand was met largely by the forced labor of enslaved Africans, predominantly of Igbo descent.

The statistics are telling and heart-wrenching. Of the 37,000 Africans trafficked to Virginia from Calabar during the 18th century, a staggering 30,000 were of Igbo descent. This figure not only highlights the scale of the trade but also underscores the significant presence of the Igbo community in the early chapters of American history.

The Mosaic of Nigerian Ethnic Groups in the Atlantic Slave Trade

The Atlantic slave trade, a dark chapter in human history, involved the forced movement of countless African individuals. Among these were members of several prominent Nigerian ethnic groups, each bringing with them a rich tapestry of culture, tradition, and resilience, which would later shape the contours of the diaspora in the New World. This piece delves deeper into the predominant ethnicities that were caught in this web of enslavement and especially focuses on the distinctive characteristics of the Igbo people.

Nigerian Ethnicities in the Shadows of Chains

Foremost among the enslaved Africans were the Igbo and Yoruba people. Hailing from the fertile lands and vibrant cultures of Nigeria, these groups found themselves disproportionately targeted and captured. Their communities, known for their intricate art, deep-rooted traditions, and organized political structures, faced a significant rupture as vast numbers were taken across the Atlantic.

Yet, the net of the slave trade cast far and wide. Alongside the Igbo and Yoruba, other ethnic groups such as the Fulani, known for their pastoralist traditions, and the Edo, with their connection to the powerful Benin Empire, were also ensnared. These groups, among others from Nigeria, collectively formed a significant portion of those who were uprooted from their homeland.

The Igbo Spirit: Resistance, Resilience, and Legacy

The Igbo people, even amidst the debilitating conditions of captivity, stood out for their indomitable spirit. This was manifest in their frequent acts of rebellion against their oppressors. Such acts were not mere displays of discontent; they were powerful assertions of their humanity against a system that sought to dehumanize them. Their resistance came at great personal cost, with many choosing the path of suicide as a final act of defiance against the chains of enslavement.

Beyond the period of the Atlantic slave trade, the footprints of the Igbo community could be traced to various parts of the United States, notably Kentucky. As settlers moved and territories expanded in the subsequent century, the Igbo, either as freed individuals or those who were still enslaved, found themselves in these new lands, shaping their narratives and communities.

Furthermore, historians have put forth compelling arguments, backed by data, that suggest that the Igbo might have also constituted the majority of slaves in Maryland. This assertion underscores the breadth of their presence and the depth of their impact in the early annals of American history.

Nigerian Diaspora in America: Migration Waves and Cultural Imprints

The intricate tapestry of America's history and culture has been woven together by waves of migrants from all corners of the world. Among these groups, the Nigerians, particularly those of Igbo descent, have carved out a unique and poignant narrative. From the forced migrations during the slave trade era to later voluntary movements seeking refuge from war, their journey tells a tale of survival, resilience, and cultural preservation.

The Echoes of War: Igbo Migration in the Late 20th Century

While the historical memory of the Atlantic slave trade is etched deeply, there's a more recent chapter that demands attention. The late 1960s witnessed significant geopolitical upheavals in Africa, with the Nigerian Civil War (also known as the Biafran War) as a key focal point. The conflict, marked by ethnic tensions and devastating humanitarian crises, led to a significant exodus of the Igbo people.

Fleeing the horrors of war, many Igbo sought refuge in various countries, and a noticeable segment made their way to the United States. This migration wave was starkly different from earlier ones. These individuals were not bound in chains; they were refugees, actively choosing the path of exodus in search of safety and a chance to rebuild their lives. Their arrival enriched the already diverse Nigerian-American community, adding another layer to its multifaceted history.

Enduring Symbols: Cultural Markers and Identity

Amid the turmoil of displacement, whether through the brutality of enslavement or the chaos of war, one constant remained for many Nigerian ethnic groups: their rich cultural heritage. A striking aspect of this heritage is the intricate tattoo and scarification designs that adorned their bodies. For groups like the Yoruba, these weren't just aesthetic choices. They bore deep significance, denoting lineage, status, and communal affiliations.

These cultural markers also served a pragmatic purpose, especially during the era of the slave trade. For those who managed the harrowing feat of escaping the clutches of their oppressors, these tattoos and scars could potentially aid in reconnecting with members of their ethnic group. The shared symbols, etched in flesh, became beacons of hope and identifiers in a land where their very identities were under threat.

Though few in number, the escaped slaves who bore these marks and managed to find kin or tribe members could derive strength, support, and perhaps even a semblance of the home they had lost. While the oppressive system sought to strip enslaved individuals of their cultural identities, these enduring symbols resisted erasure, testifying to the resilience and tenacity of the human spirit.

Cultural Suppression and the Final Acts of the Atlantic Slave Trade

America's history with slavery is marked not only by the physical chains that bound countless Africans but also by the systematic attempts to sever these individuals from their rich cultural heritages. As the dynamics of the slave trade evolved, so did the strategies of the oppressors, with cultural eradication becoming a tool of control. Parallelly, the efforts to end this heinous trade marked significant milestones in the American narrative. This exploration delves into the dark endeavors to wipe out African cultures during the slave era and the eventual, albeit belated, steps taken to end the Atlantic slave trade.

The Systematic Erasure of Identity: A Tool of Oppression

To ensure control and mitigate potential uprisings, slave owners and traders adopted a sinister strategy: stripping the enslaved of their cultural identities. By doing so, they aimed to weaken the bonds that united individuals, rendering them more vulnerable and compliant.

One of the primary tactics involved actively discouraging traditional tribal customs. These customs, which ranged from songs and dances to rituals and ceremonies, were seen as threats. They provided the enslaved with a sense of identity, a connection to their roots, and perhaps most importantly, a form of solace and resistance against their grim realities.

To further quell the chances of rebellion and hinder intra-group communication, slavers often deliberately mixed individuals from different ethnic backgrounds. The intent was clear: to create barriers of language and culture among the enslaved, making it challenging for them to unite, communicate, or plan revolts. By doing so, the oppressors aimed to create an environment of isolation and mistrust, ensuring that the enslaved remained subjugated.

A Legal End, But Not The Final Chapter

While the systemic attempts to erase African cultures persisted, voices against the Atlantic slave trade grew louder. In a significant legislative move, U.S. President Thomas Jefferson officially outlawed the trade in 1808. This marked a pivotal moment, signaling a shift in the nation's stance against a deeply entrenched and lucrative system.

However, while the law might have signaled the end of the trade on paper, reality painted a grimmer picture. Unscrupulous merchants and slave traders, lured by the potential profits, continued to smuggle enslaved Africans into the country illegally. Moreover, the institution of slavery itself persisted, casting a dark shadow over the nation. It would take the tumultuous events of the American Civil War, and the subsequent Emancipation Proclamation, to finally bring an end to this abhorrent practice in the United States.

Chapter 3 - Intergenerational Success of Nigerian Americans: Key Factors

Introduction to the Nigerian Spirit

Nigeria, a nation rich in history, diverse in its cultures, and abundant in natural resources, has long been recognized as a giant of Africa. Nestled in West Africa, it boasts a patchwork of over 250 ethnic groups, each with its unique languages, traditions, and stories. A closer examination of Nigeria's past reveals a tapestry of empires, colonial rule, struggles for independence, civil war, and a constant push for modernity against the backdrop of tradition. This intricate history has, over the centuries, cultivated a spirit of resilience and determination among its people.

The Nigerian spirit is, perhaps, best described as an undying flame of tenacity. It is rooted in the rich soils of its ancient civilizations, like the Nok, which date back to 1500 BC, and flourished through the ages with the rise of empires like the Oyo and Benin. These kingdoms, with their sophisticated administrative structures and flourishing trade routes, were a testament to the early ingenuity of the Nigerian people.

However, the true mettle of the Nigerian spirit was tested during the colonial era. The British colonizers, attracted by Nigeria's wealth, sought to control and exploit its resources, subjecting its people to decades of subjugation. Despite this, the spirit of resistance and the thirst for autonomy thrived. From the Aba Women's Riots in 1929, where women challenged colonial policies, to the relentless push for independence that came to fruition in 1960, Nigerians showcased their unwavering determination to forge their path.

Yet, the journey post-independence was fraught with challenges. The Biafra war, political instability, and economic downturns could have broken the spirit of any nation. But Nigerians, driven by their deep-rooted resilience, continued to rise, adapt, and evolve. This unyielding spirit manifests itself today in the myriad of Nigerians excelling on global platforms, from literature and arts to science and technology.

Origins of "Naija No Dey Carry Last"

"Naija No Dey Carry Last" – a phrase that resonates deeply with every Nigerian and encapsulates the ethos of a nation that refuses to be defeated. The Pidgin phrase "Naija No Dey Carry Last" can be translated as "Nigerians strive to finish first." This colloquial expression encapsulates the relentless, determined spirit and drive for excellence that is characteristic of Nigerians in various fields of endeavour.

The phrase is more than just a collection of words; it's a battle cry, a mantra that reaffirms the Nigerian belief in excellence, resilience, and an unyielding drive to succeed against all odds. While it's challenging to pinpoint the exact origins of "Naija No Dey Carry Last," it's deeply rooted in Nigerian Pidgin – a creole language born out of the interactions between local languages and the English of the colonial rulers. Pidgin, over time, has become an embodiment of Nigerian street wisdom, wit, and humor.

"Naija No Dey Carry Last" is an affirmation. It serves as a reminder of the Nigerian legacy of not settling for mediocrity. Whether it's in the bustling markets of Lagos where traders weave their magic from dawn to dusk or in the classrooms where students burn the midnight oil in pursuit of academic excellence – the sentiment is the same. Nigerians are not content with just participating; they aim to lead, to be at the forefront, to be the best.

This ethos is evident in the global accomplishments of Nigerians. Be it the literary genius of Chinua Achebe and Chimamanda Ngozi Adichie or the musical prowess of Burna Boy and Wizkid, they all embody the spirit of "Naija No Dey Carry Last." They serve as beacons of excellence, showcasing to the world that the Nigerian spirit, when set on a goal, is indomitable.

Why "Naija No Dey Carry Last" Resonates Profoundly with Nigerians

To understand why "Naija No Dey Carry Last" holds such significance for Nigerians, one must first delve into the psyche of the nation. It is a saying that transcends linguistic barriers, striking a chord in the heart of every Nigerian. Why? Because it mirrors their unwavering national pride and an unequivocal belief in the latent potential their homeland possesses.

When one navigates through Nigeria's historical tapestry, it becomes evident that the nation, though blessed with abundant natural resources and cultural riches, has faced its share of adversities. From political unrest to economic downturns, Nigeria has been tested time and again. However, instead of these challenges diminishing the Nigerian spirit, they only served to bolster it. "Naija No Dey Carry Last" became an anthem, reminding every Nigerian of their ancestors who stood tall through trials and signalling to future generations that they too possess the grit and tenacity to surmount any challenge.

Furthermore, the phrase is a homage to the core values and attributes that define Nigerians. A nation known for its diligent work ethic, boundless creativity, and a zest for life,

Nigeria continually produces individuals who leave an indelible mark on the global stage. Whether it's in literature, music, sports, or entrepreneurship, Nigerians have showcased their brilliance, time and again. And every time a Nigerian succeeds, it reaffirms the belief encapsulated in the phrase.

Additionally, "Naija No Dey Carry Last" serves as a cultural compass, guiding Nigerians, especially the younger generation, to cherish and uphold their heritage. In a world that is rapidly globalizing, it is easy for cultural identities to get diluted. However, this phrase, while emphasizing the importance of progress, also underscores the significance of staying connected to one's roots.

Strong Emphasis on Education and Professional Pursuits: The Backbone of Nigerian Immigrant Success

Education has long been revered as the key to unlocking opportunities and ensuring upward mobility in societies around the world. For Nigerian immigrant families, this belief isn't just a cultural value; it's an unwavering principle that forms the bedrock of their pursuit of success. Their emphasis on education and professional stability isn't merely a choice; it's a meticulously planned strategy that ensures both immediate and intergenerational success.

From the bustling cities of Lagos and Abuja to the serene towns nestled along the Niger River, Nigeria, with its rich cultural tapestry and diverse population, has always placed a premium on knowledge and learning. Historically, communities and families have cherished scholars, and this reverence for education has been transported across oceans, deeply ingrained within the psyche of Nigerian immigrants.

Upon setting foot on foreign shores, these immigrants often face a myriad of challenges, from cultural assimilation struggles to economic hardships. Yet, amidst these trials, one constant remains: the unwavering focus on education. The narrative isn't just about survival but thriving, and Nigerian families quickly recognize that academic accomplishments can be the catalyst for this success.

Why, one might ask, is there such an intense focus on specific fields like medicine and engineering? The answer lies in the pragmatic approach these families adopt. Medicine and engineering are not just respected professions; they represent consistency, stability, and global relevance. A doctor or engineer isn't just valued in Nigeria or the United States; their skills are in demand worldwide. In an ever-evolving global job market, these professions offer a semblance of job security that few other fields can guarantee.

Additionally, there's a broader societal perspective at play. In many communities across Nigeria, professions like medicine and engineering are often equated with success and prestige. A doctor or an engineer in the family isn't just a personal achievement; it's a collective victory, a testament to the family's dedication and hard work. Such accomplishments uplift the family's status within the community, weaving a narrative of perseverance, ambition, and success.

Children growing up in Nigerian immigrant households often hear tales of sacrifices made by their ancestors, stories of immense challenges countered by indomitable spirits. These narratives serve as powerful motivators, pushing them to achieve not just for personal growth but as a tribute to the generations that paved the way. The journey to becoming a doctor, engineer, or any other esteemed professional becomes a familial rite of passage, a path trodden by many before and a legacy to be upheld for the ones that follow.

Furthermore, the emphasis on education isn't just about professional pursuits; it's about equipping the next generation with the tools to navigate an increasingly complex world. The world is no longer bound by geographical borders, and today's challenges require global solutions. By channelling their children towards globally recognized fields, Nigerian parents ensure that their offspring are not just limited to local or national opportunities. They are, in essence, global citizens, equipped with skills and knowledge that are universally applicable.

Family-Centric Drive: The Heartbeat of Nigerian Immigrant Success

In various cultures worldwide, the family stands as the cornerstone, the anchor holding individuals together. This sentiment is deeply embedded in the ethos of Nigerian immigrants, where family isn't just an integral unit but the driving force behind many of their aspirations and endeavours. The motivation to succeed, to climb higher rungs of the socio-economic ladder, to secure a better future is not solely fuelled by individual ambition but primarily by a collective, family-centric drive.

Understanding the significance of the family in Nigerian culture requires delving deep into its historical and societal roots. In Nigeria, the notion of family extends beyond the immediate nuclear unit. It encompasses extended families, clans, and sometimes even entire communities. The successes and failures of an individual are often seen as reflective of their broader family. This interconnected sense of responsibility and shared destiny molds individuals' aspirations from a young age.

The journey of Nigerian immigrants often begins with a dream—a dream of better opportunities, a brighter future, and a prosperous life. But this dream isn't solely personal. It's a vision shared by mothers and fathers, grandparents, siblings, and sometimes even distant relatives. The decision to migrate, to leave behind the familiar terrains of Nigeria and venture into the unknown, is frequently driven by a collective ambition: to pave a golden path for the subsequent generations.

Once on foreign shores, the challenges that Nigerian immigrants encounter are manifold—cultural, financial, and emotional. Amidst the struggles of assimilation and the longing for their homeland, what keeps them grounded and continually striving is the family-centric drive. Every late-night study session, every extra work shift, every business endeavor is underpinned by a burning desire not just to succeed but to lay a foundation upon which their children and grandchildren can build. The aim is to erect a legacy of prosperity, where each successive generation can stand taller, having been hoisted up by the efforts of those who came before.

Moreover, this family-driven ethos manifests in various ways. Within Nigerian immigrant households, it's common to find multi-generational living arrangements, where grandparents, parents, and children cohabit, sharing responsibilities and pooling resources. This close-knit familial structure provides a robust support system, ensuring that individuals, whether young or old, always have a safety net to fall back on. It's a symbiotic relationship, where every member contributes to and benefits from the collective prosperity.

Another aspect of the family-centric drive is the transmission of values, traditions, and wisdom from one generation to the next. Nigerian parents often impart stories of their homeland, tales of resilience, perseverance, and ambition, to their children. These narratives, enriched with lessons from the past, serve as guiding beacons for the younger generation, instilling in them the values of hard work, respect, and community.

Practical Career Choices: The Nigerian Blueprint for Global Success

Across the world, the choices people make regarding their careers are shaped by multiple factors, from personal interests to societal expectations. However, within the Nigerian diaspora, a distinct pattern emerges, characterized by a strategic, practical approach to career selection. Driven by an understanding of the global job market and the impermanence of geopolitical situations, Nigerians frequently emphasize professions that possess high demand, consistent relevance, and universal applicability. Prominent among these are roles in medicine, engineering, and similar sectors that ensure employability across borders.

The underpinnings of this pragmatic career approach are rooted in Nigeria's history and societal fabric. As one of the most populous countries in Africa, Nigeria, with its diverse ethnic groups and multifaceted cultures, has always been a hub of ambition and aspiration. Amidst its richness, the nation has also grappled with economic challenges, political instabilities, and infrastructural deficits. This juxtaposition of immense potential and systemic hurdles has cultivated a mindset among Nigerians: the need to be equipped with skills and qualifications that are universally recognized and always in demand.

Medicine stands out as a prime example. Being a doctor isn't just seen as a noble profession but also as a practical one. The ability to heal, to alleviate suffering, is a skill that's valued everywhere, from the bustling cities of Europe and North America to the remote villages of Asia and Africa. Nigerian families, understanding this universal reverence for healthcare professionals, often encourage their children to venture into medicine. It's a career path that not only promises a respectable position in society but also offers financial stability and the flexibility to practice anywhere in the world.

Similarly, engineering, in its myriad forms, is another career avenue that's held in high regard. Engineers, with their ability to design, innovate, and build, are the backbone of any developing or developed society. Whether it's civil engineers constructing bridges and skyscrapers or software engineers driving the digital revolution, their contributions are pivotal. Recognizing the perennial need for such skills, many Nigerians prioritize engineering as a field of study and professional pursuit.

However, this practical approach to career choices isn't just about global employability. It's also about resilience and adaptability. In an ever-changing world, where economies rise and fall, and political landscapes shift, having a universally valued profession serves as a safety net. It ensures that even if circumstances change, if geopolitical tensions arise or if economic downturns strike, those equipped with skills like medicine or engineering can navigate challenges, find opportunities, and continue to prosper.

Moreover, this emphasis on universally recognized professions also fosters a sense of community and mentorship. As more Nigerians venture into fields like medicine and engineering, they lay down a pathway for those that follow, creating networks, offering guidance, and building ecosystems that nurture and support future generations.

Skepticism Towards Uncertain Professions: The Nigerian Pragmatism in Career Choices

Throughout the world, we often hear stories of individuals chasing their dreams, diving into fields driven by passion, sometimes against all odds. From the world of entertainment to the fields of sports, the allure of fame, success, and the sheer love for the craft drives many. However, within the Nigerian diaspora, there is a noticeable trend that stands somewhat juxtaposed to this global narrative. Despite having prodigious talents in areas like sports, music, or arts, many Nigerians, influenced by familial and cultural norms, gravitate towards more 'guaranteed' career paths. The reason? A deep-rooted understanding of the unpredictable and ephemeral nature of professions like athletics and entertainment.

For Nigerians, both at home and abroad, life's experiences and historical context play a pivotal role in shaping this perspective. The country, with its diverse and rich tapestry of cultures, has seen its share of challenges, from political upheavals to economic downturns. These experiences have ingrained a sense of pragmatism and a penchant for security and stability in many Nigerians.

Take sports, for instance. The world of professional athletics, while offering the allure of fame, glory, and financial rewards, is also fraught with uncertainties. An injury, a change in team management, or just the natural progression of age can dramatically alter an athlete's career trajectory. Unlike professions such as medicine, engineering, or law, success in sports often comes with an expiration date.

For many Nigerian families, investing the formative years of their children's lives in such a volatile career path can seem like a high-stakes gamble.

This isn't to say that Nigerians lack appreciation for sports or arts. On the contrary, Nigeria has a rich heritage in music, arts, and sports. Nigerian music, especially genres like Afrobeats, has gained global acclaim, and the country's sportspeople, especially footballers, have left their mark on international stages. But behind the success stories are countless tales of talented individuals whose stars faded before they could shine bright. It's these untold stories, combined with the societal emphasis on stability, that fuel the skepticism.

Additionally, the Nigerian emphasis on education further cements this perspective. The value placed on academic excellence means that from a young age, many are steered towards fields that promise not just immediate job prospects but long-term career growth. There's a prevalent belief that while talents can open doors, a solid educational foundation builds the house.

It's also worth noting that the family unit plays a significant role in this dynamic. In Nigerian culture, the family is not just a social unit but a support system, a collective that rejoices in successes and rallies during challenges. The dreams and aspirations of an individual often become intertwined with the hopes and expectations of the family. Thus, decisions about career paths are often collective, made after weighing the pros and cons and considering the long-term implications for the family unit.

Realization of American Opportunities: The Diligent Work Ethic of Nigerian Immigrants

When Nigerian immigrants set foot on American soil, they often come with dreams, aspirations, and a vision for a brighter future. These aspirations are not born from thin air; they stem from an acute realization of the vast opportunities that America, often termed the "land of the free and home of the brave," presents. The United States, with its rich tapestry of cultures, its promise of the American dream, and its history of being a melting pot of diverse backgrounds, beckons to many, including Nigerians, with the allure of potential success.

For many Nigerian immigrants, this potential is not just seen as an abstract concept but as a tangible goal. They often arrive with stories of their homeland, tales of challenges faced, and memories of a culture steeped in resilience and perseverance. These stories shape their perspective, driving them to work hard and make the most of the chances America offers.

They understand that success in this new land requires not just talent or luck, but a diligent and unyielding work ethic.

This perspective is not unique to Nigerians. History has shown that many immigrant groups, upon arriving in America, have exhibited similar traits of diligence and perseverance. A prime example is the Korean immigrant community. Like Nigerians, Koreans in America have often been noted for their tenacity, commitment to education, and a rigorous work ethic. Both communities, coming from distinct cultural backgrounds, find common ground in their approach to life in the U.S. They both recognize that while America offers opportunities aplenty, realizing one's dreams requires effort, dedication, and an unwavering commitment to one's goals.

The reasons for this diligent approach are manifold. For one, many Nigerian immigrants see their journey to America as not just a personal endeavour but a collective family mission. They bear the weight of their family's hopes and dreams, understanding that their success can pave the way for future generations. This sense of collective responsibility, coupled with the desire to make the most of American opportunities, drives them to push boundaries, often working long hours, pursuing higher education, and constantly seeking avenues for growth.

Additionally, Nigerian immigrants, much like their Korean counterparts, often come from backgrounds where the value of hard work is instilled from a young age. In Nigeria, a country with its own set of socio-economic challenges, making one's mark requires grit and determination. Transplanted to the American context, this work ethic becomes a potent force, propelling Nigerian immigrants to carve out their niche, often achieving success in fields ranging from academia and medicine to business and the arts.

However, this realization of American opportunities and the subsequent diligent approach is not without its challenges. Adapting to a new culture, facing the complexities of immigrant life, and often navigating systemic barriers can be taxing. Yet, the undying spirit, the belief in the American dream, and the commitment to hard work see many Nigerian immigrants through, allowing them to build lives they can be proud of and contribute positively to the American mosaic.

No Limits Attitude: The Unbounded Aspirations of Hard Workers in America

In the vast landscapes of America, where dreams meet opportunities and aspirations take flight, there exists an attitude that truly defines the spirit of its people and its many immigrants: the 'No Limits' attitude. This perspective is not just an approach to life but a deeply ingrained belief system that propels individuals to achieve beyond boundaries, break barriers, and continuously redefine success. For many, America is not just a country; it's an idea, a promise of limitless possibilities, where the only ceiling is the one you place on yourself.

This attitude is a product of America's rich history and foundational ethos. The stories of self-made individuals, pioneers in various fields, innovators who reshaped industries, and ordinary people achieving extraordinary feats have constantly showcased that in America, with hard work and determination, the sky's the limit. This narrative has drawn millions to its shores, searching for the elusive American dream.

For many immigrants, America represents a fresh start, a canvas waiting to be painted with their aspirations. Unlike in some parts of the world where societal structures, economic constraints, or political turmoil might stifle dreams, America offers a unique proposition. Here, irrespective of one's background, ethnicity, or past, individuals often feel that they can carve out their destiny. This potent feeling of being in control of one's fate, buoyed by countless success stories, gives birth to the 'No Limits' attitude.

One of the most compelling aspects of this attitude is its self-reinforcing nature. As individuals begin to realize their potential and achieve their goals, they set even loftier targets. Success breeds ambition, which drives individuals to work harder, seek better opportunities, and continuously push the envelope. This cycle of aspiration, achievement, and renewed aspiration ensures continuous upward mobility in terms of socio-economic status and personal growth.

Furthermore, the 'No Limits' attitude also deeply impacts communities and shapes cultures. In families, parents instill in their children the belief that they can achieve anything with dedication and effort. Schools and institutions champion the cause of dreamers, innovators, and thinkers, fostering environments where creativity and ambition are celebrated. Communities rally around their members, encouraging them to reach for the stars, reinforcing the belief that every dream is valid and attainable in America.

However, it's essential to understand that while the 'No Limits' attitude is powerful, it is not devoid of challenges. Realizing boundless dreams requires hard work, resilience, adaptability, and an unyielding spirit. There will be obstacles, setbacks, and moments of doubt. But the unwavering belief in one's potential and the relentless pursuit of one's goals differentiates dreamers from achievers.

Chapter 4: Education

Education in Nigerian Culture: A Pillar of Progress and Identity

In the vast landscape of Africa, Nigeria stands out not just for its oil reserves or diverse ethnic groups but for its profound respect for education. As the most populous country in Africa, Nigeria has a rich tapestry of cultures, traditions, and languages. At the heart of this diverse nation lies a unified belief: education is a powerful tool for individual growth and societal advancement.

Historical Roots

Historically, Nigeria has always valued knowledge. Long before the advent of colonial rule, indigenous communities had their own systems of education, teaching moral values, history, crafts, and various other essential skills required for life. The coming of Islam and

Christianity further introduced formalized systems of learning. Over time, as the nation grappled with the challenges of colonialism and the subsequent quest for independence, education became the rallying point for progress, unity, and liberation.

Symbol of Status and Pride

In Nigerian culture, education is more than just learning from books; it's a status symbol. A person's educational background often commands respect in social circles. During social gatherings, it's common for individuals to introduce themselves by mentioning their academic qualifications, as it's a mark of pride and achievement. Parents, in particular, wear their children's academic achievements as a badge of honor, and many families prioritize education above all else, often making significant sacrifices to ensure their children receive the best possible schooling.

The Doorway to Opportunities

Nigeria, like many other developing countries, faces a myriad of challenges, including poverty, unemployment, and underdevelopment. In this context, education is seen as the key to escaping the vicious cycle of poverty. With the right qualifications, individuals can access better job opportunities, command higher salaries, and improve their quality of life. Thus, education isn't just a cultural priority; it's a practical necessity. Every degree or additional degree qualification is viewed as one step closer to a brighter future.

A Means to Preserve Culture and Tradition

Nigeria is a melting pot of over 250 ethnic groups, each with its distinct language, customs, and traditions. Education plays a crucial role in preserving this rich heritage. Schools often include cultural teachings in their curriculum, ensuring that the younger generation understands and appreciates their roots. Festivals, folklore, traditional dances, and music are not just extracurricular activities; they are mediums through which history and values are passed down. In this way, education becomes the bridge between the past and the present, ensuring that Nigeria's diverse cultural identity remains intact.

Empowerment and Social Change

Education, particularly for girls and women, is a tool for empowerment in Nigeria. With a solid educational background, women can challenge societal norms, fight for their rights, and make informed decisions about their lives. They become active participants in the nation's development, shattering glass ceilings and redefining gender roles. As Malala Yousafzai famously said, "One child, one teacher, one book, and one pen can change the world." In Nigeria, this belief resonates deeply.

Moreover, education acts as a catalyst for social change. As more Nigerians become educated, they are better equipped to address societal issues, from corruption to health crises, pushing the nation towards a brighter and more prosperous future.

The Nigerian American immigrant experience:

A Focus on Higher Education

Nigerian Americans, a subset of the broader African diaspora in the United States, have carved a distinct and commendable identity in the domain of education. Statistically, Nigerian American immigrants stand out for their high educational attainment. Remarkably, they are more likely to have a college degree compared to many other immigrant groups in the U.S. Delving into the reasons behind this phenomenon provides valuable insights into the culture, values, and aspirations of this unique community.

1. Socio-cultural Emphasis on Education

The value of education is deeply embedded in Nigerian culture, as discussed earlier. This emphasis doesn't fade when Nigerians migrate to other countries. For many Nigerian families, educational success is non-negotiable. It's seen as a path to personal and familial upliftment, and often, parents make significant sacrifices to ensure their children excel academically. This cultural mindset, transferred across borders, undoubtedly contributes to the high educational achievements of Nigerian American immigrants.

2. Migration Selectivity

The process of migration, especially to a country like the U.S., is often arduous and selective. Those who migrate tend to be among the more ambitious, driven, and resourceful individuals. Nigerian immigrants to the U.S. often belong to a

A subset of the Nigerian population that already values and possesses higher education. This selection bias means that a high proportion of Nigerian immigrants may already have college degrees before their arrival or are inclined to pursue one in the U.S.

3. Overcoming Stereotypes

The global narrative is often riddled with stereotypes about Africa and its diverse nations. To counter these preconceived notions and establish a firm footing in their adopted homeland, many Nigerian Americans feel an added pressure to excel, especially in fields that command respect and credibility. Higher education becomes both a shield and a sword, defending against bias while carving out a space of recognition and respect.

4. Robust Community Networks

Nigerian American communities across the U.S. often have strong networks that emphasize mentorship and support. Older generations or more established immigrants often guide newcomers, advising them on educational pathways, scholarship opportunities, and career choices. This community-driven guidance is invaluable, offering direction and resources for newer immigrants to navigate the American educational system successfully.

5. The Drive for Socio-Economic Mobility

America, for many immigrants, is the land of opportunity. The quest for a better life often translates into socioeconomic mobility, and education is a recognized vehicle for this. Nigerian Americans understand the transformative power of a college degree in the U.S. job market and pursue higher education to enhance their chances of economic success, stability, and integration.

6. Role Models and Representation

In recent years, the success stories of numerous Nigerian Americans in diverse fields – from literature with the likes of Chimamanda Ngozi Adichie to medicine, politics, and technology – serve as inspiring examples for the community. Such visible success stories, many rooted in educational attainment, act as motivating factors for younger generations to pursue academic excellence.

Nigerian Immigrants: Shining Stars in STEM, Medicine, and Law

In the grand tapestry of global migration, Nigerian immigrants emerge as an incredible testament to resilience, ambition, and excellence. Particularly impressive is their notable presence and success in fields that demand rigorous training, precision, and dedication: STEM (Science, Technology, Engineering, and Mathematics), medicine, and law. This narrative delves into the remarkable achievements of Nigerian immigrants in these domains and unravels the factors behind their exceptional success.

1. STEM: Pioneers and Innovators

Nigerian immigrants have consistently made their mark in the world of STEM. From top tech firms like Google and Microsoft to esteemed research institutions, their contributions are tangible and transformative.

Academic Excellence: Many Nigerian immigrants in the U.S. and other Western countries often pursue degrees in engineering, computer science, and related fields. They excel in these areas, not just because of innate talent, but due to a rigorous educational foundation laid In Nigeria, where subjects like mathematics and physics are highly emphasized.

Innovation: Nigerian tech entrepreneurs are creating waves in Silicon Valley and other tech hubs around the world. Their unique perspectives, combined with top-notch technical training, position them to offer innovative solutions to global challenges.

2. Medicine: Healing and Leading

The medical field, known for its demanding training and high stakes, is another arena where Nigerian immigrants shine brightly.

Pursuit of Medical Training:

Medicine is a highly respected profession in Nigerian culture. Many families encourage their children to pursue medical careers, recognizing the profession's noble mission and the potential for socioeconomic mobility.

Excellence in Practice:

Nigerian doctors, nurses, and healthcare professionals are renowned for their dedication, expertise, and patient-centric approach. Whether they've received their initial training in Nigeria and then furthered it abroad or pursued their entire medical education overseas, their commitment to the medical profession is unwavering.

3. Law: Advocates for Justice

In the intricate world of law, Nigerian immigrants stand out for their sharp analytical skills, dedication to justice, and exceptional oratory prowess.

Legal Luminaries:

Many Nigerian immigrants have ascended to prestigious positions in the legal world, from partners in top law firms to esteemed judges. Their keen understanding of legal principles, combined with a deep commitment to ethics, sets them apart.

Champions of Rights:

Several Nigerian legal professionals have made it their mission to champion the rights of marginalized communities, not just within the diaspora but also for broader global causes. Their experiences as immigrants often shape their perspectives, making them empathetic advocates.

Factors Behind Their Success

Several elements contribute to the extraordinary achievements of Nigerian immigrants in these fields:

I. **Cultural Emphasis on Education:** As previously discussed, the Nigerian culture places immense importance on academic success. This ingrained value drives many to pursue and excel in rigorous fields.

II. **Resilience and Adaptability:** Facing the challenges of immigration and adapting to new environments hones resilience.

This strength translates to determination in professional pursuits.

III. **Community Support:** Nigerian immigrant communities often foster environments of mutual support and mentorship, guiding newcomers through the challenges of foreign educational and professional systems.

Ngozi Okonjo-Iweala: A Trailblazing Leader in Global Finance

Ngozi Okonjo-Iweala, a Nigerian-American economist and international development expert, has carved a significant niche in the realms of global finance and development. As the first female Director-General of the World Trade Organization (WTO), her tenure since 2021 has been a testament to her steadfast dedication to fostering economic growth, reducing poverty, and championing gender equality.

Early Life and Formative Years

Born in Ogwashi-Uku, Nigeria, in 1954, Okonjo-Iweala's early life laid the foundation for her future endeavors. Her passion for economics and international affairs led her to Harvard University, where she graduated with a Bachelor of Arts in Economics in 1976. She further advanced her academic pursuits at the Massachusetts Institute of Technology (MIT), earning a Master in City Planning in 1978 and a Doctor of Philosophy in Regional Economics and Development in 1981. These formative years shaped her worldview and equipped her with the tools to tackle global economic challenges.

Pioneering Role at the World Bank

Okonjo-Iweala's career trajectory took a significant leap at the World Bank. Over 25 years, she evolved from a development economist to the Managing Director for

Operations. In this capacity, she oversaw an extensive $81 billion operational portfolio across diverse regions. Her tenure at the World Bank was marked by pioneering initiatives like the Multilateral Debt Relief Initiative (MDRI) and the Global Food Crisis Response Program, reflecting her commitment to reducing poverty and fostering sustainable development.

Transformative Leadership as Nigerian Minister of Finance

In 2003, Okonjo-Iweala's journey led her back to Nigeria, where she made history as the first female Minister of Finance. Her term under President Olusegun Obasanjo was a transformative period, characterized by comprehensive economic reforms and growth. She introduced pivotal policies that restructured Nigeria's debt, enhanced revenue collection, and spurred infrastructure investment. Her instrumental role in securing debt relief for Nigeria was particularly notable, significantly alleviating the country's financial constraints.

Continued Influence and Global Recognition

Post her tenure as Finance Minister, Okonjo-Iweala continued to hold influential positions, including Chair of Gavi, the Vaccine Alliance, and Co-Chair of the African Risk Capacity. Her leadership at the World Economic Forum's Global Commission on the Economy and Climate further solidified her status as a global economic leader. In 2020, she emerged as a key figure in the fight against COVID-19 as one of the African Union's Special Envoys, mobilizing international financial support to combat the pandemic's economic impact.

Historic Appointment as Director-General of WTO

Okonjo-Iweala's election as the WTO's first female Director-General in 2021 marked a historic milestone in international trade governance. In this role, she has been pivotal in reinvigorating the WTO's agenda, focusing on crucial issues like climate change, food security, and the digital economy. Her advocacy for developing countries within the WTO framework underscores her commitment to a more inclusive and equitable global trade system.

Conclusion: A Legacy of Inspiration and Impact

Ngozi Okonjo-Iweala's career is a narrative of groundbreaking achievements and inspirational leadership. Her unwavering dedication to economic development, poverty alleviation, and gender equality has not only shaped global financial policies but also inspired countless women and aspiring leaders globally. Her legacy, characterized by her innovative approach and transformative impact, continues to influence the trajectory of global trade and development, paving the way for a more prosperous and equitable world for future generations.

Chapter 5: Hard Work and Determination

Nigerian Immigrants: Epitomes of Hard Work and Determination

The global narrative of immigration is adorned with tales of tenacity, resilience, and unwavering ambition. Among these, the story of Nigerian immigrants stands out, characterized by an indomitable spirit of hard work and determination. The reasons behind this persistent drive and the remarkable successes achieved by Nigerian immigrants provide insightful glimpses into the culture, values, and aspirations of this community.

1. Rooted in Cultural Values

In Nigeria, hard work is not merely encouraged; it's woven into the very fabric of its cultural and social ethos. The importance of diligence, resilience, and ambition is instilled from a young age. Children grow up hearing stories of ancestors and contemporaries who, through sheer willpower and effort, surmounted challenges to achieve their goals.

2. The Aspiration for Better Opportunities

Like many immigrant groups, Nigerians often enter abroad in pursuit of better opportunities, whether for education, employment, or overall quality of life. This quest is fueled by a keen awareness of the potential that foreign lands might offer and a relentless drive to seize these opportunities. The very act of migration, often fraught with challenges, demands determination, making those who undertake it inherently resilient.

3. Overcoming Stereotypes and Barriers

The global stage, unfortunately, is riddled with stereotypes and misconceptions about Africa and its diverse nations. To dispel these notions and carve a niche in foreign lands, Nigerian immigrants often feel the need to work twice as hard. This drive to excel and debunk biases amplifies their inherent determination.

4. Strong Sense of Community and Mutual Upliftment

Nigerian immigrant communities, whether in the U.S., UK, or elsewhere, are tight-knit groups. There's a shared understanding that lifting one member can pave the way for others. Success stories are celebrated, and tales of hard work and achievement serve as motivational blueprints for younger generations. This environment fosters competition, yes, but more importantly, it cultivates a culture of relentless effort.

5. Value of Education and Professional Achievement

Nigeria, with its competitive educational system, instills the importance of academic and professional excellence early on. For many

Nigerians, success in these arenas is not just a personal achievement but a source of pride for their families and communities. This deeply-rooted value travels with them, making Nigerian immigrants among the most educated and determined professional groups in many countries.

6. Resilience in the Face of Adversity

Historical and socio-economic challenges in Nigeria, ranging from political unrest to economic hardships, have imbued its people with remarkable resilience. This resilience translates into an ability to face setbacks head-on, adapt to new environments, and always push forward toward their goals.

Stories of Triumph: Nigerian Immigrants Overcoming Adversity

The narrative of immigration is often one of challenge and resilience, and among its chapters, the tales of Nigerian immigrants hold a special place. Bound by an unwavering spirit, many have navigated hardships, breaking barriers to etch stories of remarkable success. Here are five such luminaries from the Nigerian diaspora:

1. Chimamanda Ngozi Adichie: The renowned author, known globally for her impactful novels like "Half of a Yellow Sun" and "Americana," arrived in the U.S. at 19. Navigating the nuances of being a Black African in America, Adichie faced cultural adjustments and battled stereotypes. Her experiences deeply influenced her writing, which often explores themes of identity, diaspora, and feminism. Today, Adichie isn't just a celebrated author but also an influential voice on global platforms, championing the causes of gender equality and cultural understanding.

2. Hakeem Olajuwon: Olajuwon's journey from Lagos to becoming one of the NBA's greatest centers is nothing short of remarkable. Arriving in the U.S. for college, he faced cultural shocks and the challenges of adapting to a new brand of basketball. However, with his unmatched work ethic and natural talent, Olajuwon led the Houston Rockets to two NBA championships and was inducted into the Basketball Hall of Fame.

3. Dr. Bennet Omalu: Omalu's story was so compelling it inspired the movie "Concussion" starring Will Smith. Arriving in the U.S. with dreams of making a difference, Dr. Omalu faced adversity in the form of backlash from the NFL when he discovered and publicized the link between American football and CTE (chronic traumatic encephalopathy). Despite powerful opposition, his determination brought this critical issue to the forefront, revolutionizing player safety in the sport.

4. Wale Adeyemo: Adeyemo's tale is one of politics and policy. Born in Nigeria and raised in the U.S., he overcame the challenges of cultural integration to become a pivotal figure in American economic policy. Adeyemo served as Deputy National Security Advisor for International Economics and is now the Deputy Secretary of the U.S. Department of the Treasury. His success underscores the potential of immigrants to shape their adopted homeland's policies and future.

Oyekunle Ayinde "Kunle" Olukotun:

An Inspiration for Nigerians in the Americas

Oyekunle Ayinde "Kunle" Olukotun's journey, from his British-Nigerian roots to becoming a pioneer in computer science, is a remarkable testament to the indomitable spirit of ambition and perseverance. As Nigerian Americans and, indeed, all immigrants in the Americas look for inspiration, Olukotun's story shines as a beacon, reminding us that our dreams, no matter how vast, are attainable.

Born in Britain to Nigerian parents, Kunle's lineage is steeped in the rich and diverse traditions of Nigeria, a country known for its vibrant cultures, resilience, and an intrinsic spirit of entrepreneurship. This heritage, combined with the opportunities and challenges of growing up in a Western country, uniquely positioned him to navigate the world with a global perspective.

As he grew, Kunle's dedication to academic excellence led him to the hallowed halls of Stanford University. Here, he not only earned the revered title of the Cadence Design Systems Professor at the Stanford School of Engineering but also became a Professor of Electrical Engineering and Computer Science. Moreover, his leadership qualities shone bright as he took charge of the Stanford Pervasive Parallelism

Lab. In a world where technology is rapidly evolving, Kunle recognized the need for parallelism in computing. His foresight and innovative thinking crowned him as the "father of the multi-core processor." Spearheading the Stanford Hydra Chip Multiprocessor research, he became instrumental in crafting the world's first general-purpose multi-core CPU. But Olukotun's journey was not just about groundbreaking inventions; it was about challenging the status quo and pushing boundaries. His work in pioneering single-chip multiprocessor, multi-threaded processor design, advancing multicore CPUs and GPUs, revolutionizing transactional memory technology, and innovating domain-specific language programming models has reshaped our technological landscape. Each of these accomplishments is not just a notch in his belt but a step forward for the entire field of computer science. For Nigerian-Americans and other immigrant communities in the Americas, Kunle's achievements serve as a powerful reminder. They remind us that our origins, no matter how humble or geographically distant, should not and do not define our potential. Instead, it is our passion, dedication, and relentless pursuit of our goals that carve our paths. The essence of Kunle's journey is deeply relatable to every immigrant. It's the story of balancing two worlds, drawing strength from one's roots, and leveraging the opportunities of the adopted homeland. His success is a testament to the fact that when equipped with the right education, environment, and ethos, there's no challenge insurmountable. However, beyond the accolades and the inventions, Kunle's story is also about giving back. Through his research, he has opened doors for countless others, mentoring the next generation of thinkers, innovators, and leaders. His commitment to fostering growth in computer architecture, scalable parallel systems, parallel programming environments, domain-specific languages, and high-level compilers ensures that the future remains bright, not just for technology but for all those who dare to dream.

The Pillars of Success: The Role of Family and Community in Uplifting Nigerian Immigrants

The tales of Nigerian immigrants achieving remarkable success in various fields around the globe often echo a common thread: the unwavering support of family and community. These two pillars, deeply rooted in Nigerian culture and values, play a pivotal role in shaping the trajectories of many immigrants, providing them with both a safety net and a springboard to soar.

1. The Bedrock of Family:

In Nigerian culture, the family is not just a social unit but an intricate network of shared responsibilities, mutual respect, and boundless support. Several facets of this familial bond underscore the success of Nigerian immigrants:

Moral and Ethical Foundations: Nigerian families instill a strong set of values in their members from a young age. Respect for elders, the importance of integrity, and the value of hard work are all principles that are deeply embedded. When Nigerian immigrants face the challenges and temptations of a new culture, these foundational morals often guide their decisions, helping them navigate unfamiliar terrain with dignity and purpose.

Emphasis on Education: Within many Nigerian families, education is revered. Parents, even those with minimal formal education themselves, often emphasize the importance of academic excellence to their children. This emphasis results in a drive to seek scholarships, attend top institutions, and excel academically, laying a strong foundation for professional success.

Financial Support: While many Nigerian immigrants arrive in foreign lands with limited financial resources, families often pool resources to support one member's overseas journey, with the understanding that this individual will later assist others in turn. This cycle of mutual financial upliftment plays a crucial role in ensuring that economic challenges do not impede the aspirations of many Nigerian immigrants.

2. The Strength of Community:

Beyond the immediate family, the broader Nigerian community, both in the homeland and within diasporas, acts as a robust support system for immigrants.

Networking Opportunities: Nigerian immigrant communities, especially in countries with significant diaspora populations, offer invaluable networking opportunities. From job referrals to partnerships in entrepreneurial ventures, these community networks can significantly eases the professional journey of newcomers.

Cultural Preservation: Adapting to a new culture while trying to preserve one's own can be challenging. Nigerian communities abroad often organize cultural events, festivals, and gatherings, providing immigrants, especially the younger generation, a sense of belonging, and a connection to their roots.

Mentorship: More established Nigerian immigrants often take on mentoring roles for newcomers, guiding them through the intricacies of foreign systems, whether educational, professional, or social. This mentor-mentee relationship often fostered within community spaces, can be pivotal in avoiding pitfalls and accelerating success.

Mutual Aid Societies: Many Nigerian communities establish formal or informal groups dedicated to assisting members in times of need. Whether it's pooling resources for medical emergencies, supporting a member's business venture, or assisting with academic fees, these mutual aid societies exemplify the spirit of community upliftment.

The Synergy of Family and Community:

While family provides the initial layer of support, the broader community often extends this safety net. The two entities work in tandem. For instance, families introduce young members to community gatherings, ensuring cultural transmission. Similarly, community networks might support individual families during crises, understanding that each family's success strengthens the community as a whole.

The remarkable success stories of Nigerian immigrants, scattered across various continents and professional fields, are often traced back to the nurturing roots of family and community. These foundational support systems, while deeply rooted in Nigerian culture, have adapted to function effectively in diaspora settings. They not only offer practical assistance but also play a psychological role, reminding every Nigerian immigrant that they are not alone in their journey.

In a world that often perceives immigration through the lenses of challenges and barriers, the Nigerian narrative shines a light on the strength of collective upliftment. As current and future generations of Nigerian immigrants continue to make their mark globally, family and community roles remain unsung. Heroes silently but surely propel each individual to their pinnacle of success.

Uzodinma Iweala: A Writer Bridging Cultures

Uzodinma Iweala stands as a Nigerian-American author, physician, and essayist whose work has profoundly impacted the literary world. His narratives, rich in themes of identity, culture, and belonging, offer a unique lens into the experiences of individuals navigating the complexities of diverse cultural environments.

Early Life: A Foundation of Cultural Duality

Born in Washington, D.C., in 1982, to Nigerian parents, Iweala's early years were marked by a life split between Nigeria and the United States. This bicultural upbringing imbued him with a deep appreciation for both Nigerian and American cultures, significantly shaping his literary perspective and global understanding.

Educated at St. Albans School in Washington, D.C., Iweala distinguished himself academically and nurtured a burgeoning passion for writing. He continued his education at Harvard University, majoring in English and American literature, where he earned prestigious awards for his outstanding undergraduate thesis.

Literary Career: Reflecting a Multifaceted Worldview

Iweala burst onto the literary scene in 2005 with his debut novel, "Beasts of No Nation." A powerful narrative set against the backdrop of the Nigerian Civil War, the novel follows the harrowing journey of a child soldier. It garnered critical acclaim, winning the Anisfield-Wolf Book Award and the Commonwealth Writers' Prize for Best First Book (Africa).

His subsequent novel, "Never Look Away," further cemented his status in the literary world, weaving a complex tale of family and identity within a Nigerian-American context. Iweala's essays and articles, featured in prominent publications like The New Yorker, The Atlantic, and Granta, delve into critical issues of race, immigration, and the African diaspora.

A Parallel Path in Medicine

Parallel to his literary achievements, Iweala pursued a medical degree, graduating from Columbia University College of Physicians and Surgeons in 2011. His medical career, particularly his residency in internal medicine, has provided him with a unique perspective on healthcare and humanity, themes often reflected in his writings.

Entrepreneurial Endeavors: Amplifying African Voices

Iweala's entrepreneurial spirit led him to co-found Ventures Africa, a platform dedicated to covering business, policy, culture, and innovation in Africa. Ventures Africa has emerged as a significant voice for African entrepreneurs, amplifying stories and ideas from the continent to a global audience.

Accolades and Recognitions

Iweala's diverse contributions have earned him numerous accolades, including the Radcliffe Institute for Advanced Study Fellowship and the Rhodes Scholarship, highlighting his excellence in both literature and academia.

Legacy: Bridging Worlds Through Words and Actions

Uzodinma Iweala's legacy transcends his achievements as an author and physician. His work bridges cultural divides, fostering understanding and empathy across communities. He serves as an inspiration to aspiring writers, medical professionals, and entrepreneurs, exemplifying the impact of dedication, creativity, and a commitment to positive change. His multifaceted career is a testament to the power of embracing one's heritage while contributing to a broader global narrative.

Chapter 6: Entrepreneurship

Entrepreneurial Spirit Unbound: The High Rate of Entrepreneurship Among Nigerian Immigrants

In the global realm of entrepreneurship, Nigerian immigrants hold a distinct and enviable reputation. They are often recognized not just for their significant representation in entrepreneurial ventures but also for the success and impact of their businesses. But what fuels this fiery entrepreneurial spirit among Nigerian immigrants? Let's delve deeper, sprinkling the exploration with exemplary tales that capture the essence of this phenomenon.

1. Rooted in Cultural Values:

Nigeria, often dubbed the 'Giant of Africa,' has a deep-seated culture of trade, business, and self-respect. Many Nigerians grow up in environments where they are exposed to family-run businesses, trading, and negotiations, embedding commercial acumen in them from an early age.

Example: Consider the bustling markets of Lagos, where even as children, many assist their families in selling goods, learning the nuances of commerce firsthand.

2. Necessity and Adaptability:

For many Nigerian immigrants, entrepreneurship is not just a choice but a response to necessity. Facing challenges like credential recognition or barriers in conventional employment sectors, many turn to starting their own ventures, capitalizing on their skills and passions.

Example: A Nigerian engineer, unable to secure a job in his field due to credential discrepancies, might launch a tech startup, channeling his expertise innovatively.

3. Community Support and Networks:

Nigerian immigrant communities, with their strong bonds and mutual support ethos, often act as springboards for budding entrepreneurs. From pooling resources to offering a ready customer base, these communities foster a conducive environment for business growth.

Example: A Nigerian immigrant launching a restaurant with authentic Nigerian cuisine can bank on the local Nigerian diaspora for initial patronage, word-of-mouth publicity, and even financial support.

4. Education and Skillset:

A significant proportion of Nigerian immigrants are highly educated. This, combined with the Nigerian emphasis on excellence and hard work, equips them with both the technical know-how and the soft skills necessary for entrepreneurial success.

Example: Chimamanda Ngozi Adichie, although primarily known as an author, utilized her educational background and skills to create a writing workshop in Nigeria, fostering new talent and filling a niche need.

5. Global Perspective:

Having experienced the dynamics of both Nigerian and foreign markets, these immigrants often possess a broader, more adaptable business perspective. They can identify gaps, needs, and opportunities that might be overlooked by others.

Example: A fashion entrepreneur might merge Western styles with traditional Nigerian patterns, appealing to a global clientele searching for unique, cross-cultural attire.

6. Resilience and Perseverance:

The journey from Nigeria to foreign lands, laden with challenges and adjustments, inherently cultivates resilience. This resilience, when translated to the business realm, results in tenacity, risk-taking, and an undeterred spirit, essential for entrepreneurial success.

Example: Facing initial rejections or setbacks, Nigerian immigrant entrepreneurs, instead of retreating, might pivot their business models, innovate, and push forward with even greater vigor.

The high rate of entrepreneurship among Nigerian immigrants is no mere coincidence. It's a confluence of cultural values, adaptability, education, community support, and global perspectives, and unyielding resilience. These entrepreneurs don't contribute to economies; they bridge cultures, create value, and stand as inspirations for both their home and adopted communities.

The stories of Nigerian immigrant entrepreneurs are not just tales of business acumen but narratives of human spirit, innovation, and a relentless drive. In an ever-globalizing world, they serve as reminders of the boundless possibilities that arise when passion meets perseverance.

The Rising Sun: Success of Nigerian-owned Businesses in the United States

The success narrative of Nigerian-owned businesses in the United States is not just a business story but a testament to adaptability, resilience, and the unique flair of blending two vibrant cultures. From tech start-ups to restaurants and from fashion brands to entertainment ventures, Nigerian entrepreneurs in the U.S. have painted the entrepreneurial landscape with strokes of innovation and authenticity. Let's embark on a journey to spotlight some of these successes.

1. Tech and Innovation:

Silicon Valley and other tech hubs have seen the rise of several Nigerian innovators, leveraging cutting-edge technology to offer solutions for both American and global markets.

Example: Dara Oladosu, the creator of Quoted Replies, a bot that helps Twitter users find quoted comments on tweets, gained international recognition, and showcased the talent emerging from Nigeria and making waves in the U.S.

2. Food and Culinary Ventures:

Nigerian cuisine, with its rich flavors and diverse offerings, has found a niche but growing audience in the U.S. Entrepreneurs have brilliantly adapted traditional recipes to cater to American palettes while retaining their authenticity.

Example: Tunde Wey, a chef from Lagos, opened his pop-up restaurant in New Orleans, focusing on Nigerian delicacies. His venture garnered attention not just for its culinary offerings but also for spotlighting issues like racial wealth disparity through dynamic pricing.

3. Fashion and Design:

African prints, especially from Nigeria, have influenced global fashion trends. Nigerian entrepreneurs in the U.S. have capitalized on this, introducing unique designs that blend Traditional Nigerian aesthetics with contemporary American styles.

Example: The brand 'Maki Oh' by Amaka Osakwe has gained international acclaim and has been worn by celebrities like Michelle Obama and Rihanna. The brand seamlessly fuses Nigerian motifs with modern silhouettes.

4. Health and Wellness:

Many Nigerian professionals in the medical field have not only excelled in their roles but have also ventured into establishing health facilities, research centers, and wellness clinics.

Example: Dr. Olaokun Soyinka, who has roots in Nigeria, founded a healthcare center in the U.S., focusing on holistic care and serving diverse communities with a special emphasis on understanding cultural nuances.

5. Entertainment and Media:

The rich tapestry of Nigerian arts, stories, and music has found representation in the U.S. entertainment industry, with entrepreneurs launching production houses, music labels, and more.

Example: David Oyelowo, a British-Nigerian actor, after his success in Hollywood, launched his production company, focusing on narratives that bridge African and Western cultures. His ventures have introduced many to the beauty and depth of Nigerian stories.

6. E-commerce and Retail:

With the digital revolution, several Nigerian entrepreneurs have delved into e-commerce, setting up platforms that cater to specific niches, often intertwining Nigerian products or ethos with American consumer needs.

Example: 'Mall for Africa,' an e-commerce platform, was founded by Chris Folayan, a Nigerian in the U.S. The platform allows Africans to purchase items directly from U.S. and UK retailers seamlessly, bridging a significant market gap.

The trajectory of Nigerian-owned businesses in the United States speaks volumes about the entrepreneurial spirit, creativity, and sheer determination of Nigerians abroad. These ventures, while contributing significantly to the U.S. economy, also play a crucial role in cultural exchange, fostering understanding and appreciation for Nigerian culture, values, and traditions.

In a broader sense, the success of these businesses paints a vivid picture: when diverse cultures intertwine in the realm of commerce, the result is not just economic prosperity but a rich mosaic of shared stories, experiences, and innovations. The narrative of Nigerian businesses in the U.S. is an ongoing one, promising more inspiration, more success, and more bridges built in the future.

Unlocking the Secret: Factors Behind the Entrepreneurial Success in Nigerian Immigrants

The undeniable entrepreneurial prowess of Nigerian immigrants, particularly evident in their ventures abroad, prompts the question: What drives this success? While there is no single answer, a mosaic of cultural, educational, and personal factors can be pieced together to explain this phenomenon. Let's delve into the primary catalysts that have contributed to the entrepreneurial triumphs of Nigerian immigrants.

1. Strong Educational Foundation:

Many Nigerian families place a high premium on education. This emphasis results in a population that is, by a significant fraction, highly educated. Such a strong foundation not only provides them with technical knowledge but also instills confidence and ambition.

Example: It's common to find Nigerian immigrants with multiple degrees or advanced qualifications, equipping them with a solid foundation to venture into entrepreneurial pursuits.

2. Cultural Values:

Growing up in Nigeria often means absorbing core values of resilience, adaptability, and a drive to succeed. The importance of community, mutual support, and a shared sense of responsibility is deeply embedded, and these values often translate into business ethics and practices.

Example: Nigerian markets and local businesses, where negotiation, relationship-building, and trust are pivotal, serve as early training grounds for many budding entrepreneurs.

3. Diaspora Networks:

Upon immigrating, Nigerian entrepreneurs can tap into expansive diaspora networks. These communities offer support, mentorship, and sometimes even capital. More than just a safety net, they serve as a springboard, propelling businesses forward.

Example: Nigerian business forums and associations abroad frequently host events, workshops, and networking sessions, fostering connections and collaborations.

4.Resilience and Determination:

Facing challenges head-on and emerging stronger is a trait many Nigerian immigrants possess. Whether it's adapting to a new culture, overcoming language barriers, or navigating unfamiliar terrains, their innate resilience often becomes their biggest business asset.

Example: Initial setbacks or business failures do not deter them; instead, they use these experiences as stepping stones towards greater success.

5.Global Perspective:

Having experienced life in Nigeria and their adopted countries, these entrepreneurs possess a unique dual perspective. They can identify needs, gaps, and opportunities in markets that others might overlook.

Example: Many Nigerian-owned businesses in the U.S. cater to both local American audiences and the African diaspora, tapping into diverse consumer needs.

6.Passion and Purpose:

Many Nigerian immigrants embark on entrepreneurial journeys not just for economic gains but driven by a deeper sense of purpose. Whether it's showcasing Nigerian culture, addressing community needs, or bridging gaps, their ventures often carry a heartbeat of passion.

Example: Numerous Nigerian entrepreneurs in the arts and entertainment sectors aim to share their rich cultural heritage with global audiences.

7.Versatility and Adaptability:

Being able to pivot, adapt, and evolve is crucial in the dynamic world of business. The multi-faceted experiences of Nigerian immigrants often make them versatile entrepreneurs, able to navigate changes with agility.

Example: Amidst the COVID-19 pandemic, many Nigerian-owned businesses swiftly transitioned to digital platforms, offering online services and virtual engagements.

The entrepreneurial success of Nigerian immigrants is not merely a result of external factors or favorable circumstances. It is a symphony of their cultural ethos, education, resilience, passion, and adaptability. As these entrepreneurs weave their dreams into the fabric of global economies, they do more than just business; they narrate tales of determination, of bridging worlds, and of the boundless potential that lies in every dreamer who dares to soar.

Adebayo Ogunlesi: A Visionary Leader in Global Infrastructure

Adebayo Ogunlesi, a Nigerian-born American investment banker and lawyer, has emerged as a preeminent figure in the world of global infrastructure. As the Chairman and Managing Partner of Global Infrastructure Partners (GIP), he has played a pivotal role in shaping the firm into one of the foremost infrastructure investment entities worldwide. Ogunlesi's influence extends beyond finance; he is also a highly respected philanthropist and civic leader, contributing significantly to various societal and cultural spheres.

Educational Foundation and Early Career

Born in Lagos, Nigeria, in 1953, Ogunlesi laid the groundwork for his future accomplishments at Oxford University, earning a Bachelor of Arts degree in philosophy, politics, and economics. He further honed his skills and knowledge at Harvard Law School, where he received his Juris Doctor degree. Post-graduation, Ogunlesi embarked on his professional journey in investment banking with Credit Suisse First Boston (CSFB), setting the stage for his future ventures.

The Genesis of Global Infrastructure Partners (GIP)

In 2006, Ogunlesi founded GIP, marking a significant milestone in his career. Under his stewardship, GIP has grown to manage over $80 billion in assets, investing in diverse infrastructure assets, including airports, roads, railways, power plants, and renewable energy projects. The firm's success under his leadership is a testament to his strategic vision and expertise in identifying and capitalizing on lucrative investment opportunities.

Steering GIP to New Heights

Ogunlesi's role at GIP is characterized by his strategic foresight, exceptional negotiation skills, and a deep commitment to sustainable development. His approach to infrastructure investment combines keen market insights with a dedication to long-term, sustainable growth, making GIP a respected name in the global financial sector.

Philanthropy and Civic Contributions

Beyond the realm of finance, Ogunlesi is an active philanthropist and civic leader. He serves as the Chairman of the Board of Trustees of the Brookings Institution and holds positions on the boards of the University of Oxford, the American Museum of Natural History, and the New York Public Library. His involvement in these institutions reflects his commitment to education, cultural preservation, and public policy.

Accolades and Recognition

Ogunlesi's contributions to finance and society have earned him wide recognition. He has been named one of Bloomberg Markets' "100 Most Influential People in Finance" and The Black Enterprise's "50 Most Influential Black Business Leaders." Additionally, he has been honored with the Nigerian National Order of Merit, the highest national recognition for achievements in public service.

Conclusion: A Legacy of Leadership and Impact

Adebayo Ogunlesi's journey from Lagos to the pinnacle of global infrastructure investment is a narrative of visionary leadership, strategic brilliance, and a steadfast commitment to making a positive impact. His legacy is not just in the successful management of billions in assets, but also in his contributions to philanthropy and civic engagement. Ogunlesi continues to inspire aspiring business leaders and entrepreneurs around the world, demonstrating the profound influence one individual can have on both the financial world and society at large.

Tope Awotona

In the world of technology and innovation, few stories are as inspiring as that of Tope Awotona, the Nigerian-American entrepreneur who turned a simple idea into a billion-dollar business. Awotona is the founder and CEO of Calendly, a scheduling software company that has revolutionized the way professionals and organizations manage their appointments and meetings. Born in Lagos, Nigeria, and immigrating to the United States as a teenager, Awotona's journey from a determined immigrant to a celebrated tech mogul encapsulates the essence of the American dream while highlighting the contributions of

Nigerian-Americans to the fabric of global entrepreneurship. Before Calendly became a household name in the tech industry, Awotona's path was paved with challenges and learning experiences. With a background as a salesman for tech firms, including EMC (now Dell EMC), Awotona experienced firsthand the inefficiencies and frustrations of scheduling meetings through back-and-forth emails. This personal frustration sparked the idea for Calendly, leading him to envision a platform that could streamline the scheduling process by allowing individuals to easily book meetings based on mutual availability, thus eliminating the need for endless email exchanges. Awotona's entrepreneurial spirit was not newfound; prior to founding Calendly, he had ventured into several business endeavors. These included selling projectors and garden tools, experiences that, although not successful, imbued him with crucial lessons on perseverance, innovation, and the importance of identifying and solving real-world problems. These early failures served as stepping stones, preparing Awotona for the monumental success that Calendly would become. Calendly's journey from a startup to a tech powerhouse is a testament to Awotona's resilience and business acumen. Initially bootstrapping the company, he managed to grow Calendly without significant external funding for years. This approach allowed him to maintain control and steadily build the product according to his vision. However, recognizing the potential for exponential growth, Awotona eventually secured a $350 million investment in 2021, which catapulted Calendly's valuation to $3 billion. This investment was not just a financial boost but a validation of Awotona's relentless pursuit of excellence and innovation. As of March 7, 2024, Tope Awotona's real-time net worth is estimated at $1.4 billion, ranking him #2147 in the world, according to Forbes. This remarkable achievement places him among the elite ranks of billionaires globally and underscores the significant impact of Calendly in the tech ecosystem. The platform's intuitive design, ease of use, and scalability have made it indispensable for millions of users worldwide, from freelancers and small business owners to large corporations. Awotona's story is a beacon of inspiration for aspiring entrepreneurs, especially those from immigrant backgrounds. His journey underscores the importance of resilience, the willingness to learn from failure, and the relentless pursuit of solving practical problems through technology. As Calendly continues to grow and evolve, Awotona's legacy as a Nigerian-American entrepreneur who dared to dream big and transform a personal frustration into a global solution cements his place in the annals of successful business leaders. Furthermore, Awotona's inclusion in Forbes' Billionaires list in 2023 is not just a personal accolade but a recognition of the broader contributions of Nigerian-Americans to entrepreneurship and innovation. His success story is a powerful reminder of the diverse talents and perspectives that immigrants bring to their adopted countries, enriching the entrepreneurial landscape and driving forward the global economy. In summary, Tope Awotona's journey from a struggling entrepreneur to the CEO of a billion-dollar tech company exemplifies the transformative power of innovation, perseverance, and strategic thinking. Through Calendly, Awotona has not only simplified scheduling but has also demonstrated the vast potential of Nigerian-American entrepreneurs to impact the world positively. His story is a testament to the idea that with determination and a focus on solving real-world problems, anyone can turn their dreams into reality.

Chapter 7: Cultural Values

Cultural Values - The Pillars of Success for Nigerian Immigrants

In the vast narrative of immigrant successes, Nigerian immigrants have consistently emerged as a shining beacon. Beyond just individual grit and determination, the cultural tapestry of Nigeria has woven intrinsic values into its people. These values, deeply rooted and carried across shores, have been instrumental in charting the success stories of Nigerian immigrants. This chapter delves into these core cultural values and their transformative impact.

1.Respect for Education:

Education in Nigerian culture is seen not merely as a step to a professional career but as a symbol of prestige and respect. Families invest heavily, both emotionally and financially, in ensuring that their children receive quality education.

Impact: This deep-rooted respect for education means many Nigerian immigrants are well-educated, creating a foundation for their success in various professional fields.

2.Family and Community Ties:

The Igbo adage, "Ora naazunwa," which means it takes a village to raise a child, encapsulates the emphasis Nigerian culture places on family and community. The success of one individual is seen as a collective achievement.

Impact: This interconnectedness provides a support system for Nigerian immigrants, fostering networks of mentorship, collaboration, and mutual assistance.

3. Resilience and Perseverance:

Nigeria's history, filled with challenges ranging from colonialism to political instability, has imbued its people with unparalleled resilience. Facing adversity with hope and determination is almost a cultural trait.

Impact: This resilience translates into tenacity in business ventures, where Nigerian immigrants persist despite setbacks, always seeking solutions and pathways to success.

4. Respect for Elders and Authority:

Elders in Nigerian culture is revered and seen as sources of wisdom and guidance. This respect for authority figures extends to teachers, community leaders, and professionals.

Impact: This value translates into strong mentor-mentee relationships in professional settings, allowing Nigerian immigrants to gain insights, guidance, and direction from seasoned individuals in their respective fields.

5. Entrepreneurial Spirit:

From bustling markets in Lagos to local trades in rural areas, the spirit of entrepreneurship is deeply ingrained in the Nigerian psyche. There's a cultural inclination to seek out opportunities, innovate, and take calculated risks.

Impact: Many Nigerian immigrants channel this entrepreneurial drive in their adopted countries, establishing businesses and ventures that thrive and contribute significantly to their new communities.

6. Value for Heritage and Identity:

Despite the myriad ethnic groups and languages in Nigeria, there's a strong attachment to one's roots, traditions, and identity. Festivals, music, stories, and art play a crucial role in preserving and celebrating this rich heritage.

Impact: By infusing their ventures with elements of their culture, Nigerian immigrants introduce unique, authentic flavors into mainstream markets, be it in entertainment, fashion, or culinary arts.

7. Integrity and Honor:

In many Nigerian communities, one's word is their bond. Integrity, honor, and trustworthiness are highly prized, with personal and family honor often at stake in business and professional dealings.

Impact: Nigerian immigrants often stand out for their commitment to their word, building trust in business and professional relationships, which in turn fosters lasting partnerships and collaboration.

Family, Community, and Education: The Cornerstones of Nigerian Culture

Nigeria, often referred to as the "Giant of Africa," is not just a land rich in resources but also a mosaic of cultures, traditions, and values. Among the myriad facets of its vibrant culture, three elements stand out in their profound influence on the ethos and character of its people: family, community, and education. These are not just concepts but lived experiences, guiding principles, and the very fabric of Nigerian society.

1. Family: The Epicenter of Life

In Nigeria, family is paramount. It is the lens through which the world is perceived, understood, and engaged with. The family isn't just about immediate relatives; it extends to a broad network of cousins, aunts, uncles, and even distant kin.

Nurturing Bonds: Family gatherings, celebrations, and communal decision- making emphasize the interconnectedness of each member. The success of one individual is celebrated as a collective achievement, while challenges are faced together.

Guidance and Mentorship: Elders in the family are respected and often play pivotal roles in guiding younger generations. Their wisdom and experiences offer invaluable life lessons, shaping the choices and aspirations of the youth.

2. Community: A Collective Strength

The famous African proverb, "It takes a village to raise a child," finds its truest embodiment in Nigerian communities. There's a shared sense of responsibility, camaraderie, and mutual support.

I. **Community Support:** Whether it's contributing to a community project, assisting in local ceremonies, or supporting a neighbor in times of need, the community stands as a united front. It's common to find communal self-help projects, locally known as "na our work," that emphasize mutual growth and progress.

II. **Cultural Preservation:** Community festivals, dances, and oral narratives play a crucial role in preserving the rich heritage of Nigeria's various ethnic groups. These events also foster a sense of identity and pride among community members.

3. Education: The Path to Prestige

In Nigerian culture, education is often regarded as the most potent tool for personal and societal advancement.

I. **Investment in the Future:** Many Nigerian families prioritize education. Achievements, sometimes even at great personal and financial sacrifices. A well-educated child is often viewed as a source of pride and a testament to the family's future prospects.

II. **Holistic Growth:** Beyond academic achievements, education is seen as a holistic journey. Moral education, respect for elders, and understanding one's cultural and societal roles are integral aspects of the learning process.

III. **Social Mobility:** For many Nigerians, education is the passport to better opportunities and upward social mobility. It's common to hear phrases like "education is the legacy" in Nigerian households, emphasizing its transformative potential.

The intricate dance between family, community, and education creates a harmonious rhythm that defines the Nigerian way of life. It offers a framework of support, a sense of belonging, and a path to achievement. For Nigerians, no matter where they are in the world, these cultural cornerstones remain a touchstone, grounding them in their roots while propelling them toward the future. As the world continues to evolve in its globalized narrative, the lessons from Nigerian culture, in the strength of its families, the unity of its communities, and the reverence for education offer timeless wisdom.

The Guiding North Star: How Nigerian Cultural Values Propel Success in the United States

As the tapestry of the American dream unfolds, we witness a spectrum of narratives. Among these, the stories of Nigerian immigrants stand out, not just for their commendable achievements but for the unique cultural arsenal they bring to the fore. The triad of family, community, and education, deeply embedded in Nigerian ethos, has been instrumental in shaping their success trajectory in the United States.

1. Family: The Pillar of Strength

For Nigerian immigrants, the family is both an anchor and a compass. Its significance transcends mere emotional bonds and plays a critical role in their pursuit of success.

Emotional and Financial Support: Venturing into the unknown terrains of a new country, the family provides a sense of continuity, stability, and emotional grounding. Moreover, many Nigerian immigrants receive financial backing from their families, aiding in initial setups for higher education or business ventures.

Legacy and Expectation: The emphasis on family honor and reputation serves as a motivating factor. Striving to succeed becomes not just a personal endeavor but a bid to uphold and enhance the family's legacy.

2. Community: An Extended Network

Nigerians are inherently communal, and this attribute seamlessly finds its place even in the vast and diverse landscape of the United States.

Networking and Collaboration: Nigerian communities often form associations and groups in the U.S., facilitating networking, exchange of resources, and mutual assistance. For instance, professional associations of Nigerians in various fields can offer guidance, mentorship, and sometimes even job opportunities.

Solidarity in Adversity: The communal mindset fosters a culture of shared responsibilities. Whether it's pooling resources for a business venture, guiding newcomers through the maze of U.S. bureaucracy, or offering emotional support during challenging times, the community becomes a dependable bedrock.

3. Education: The Key to Opportunities

The reverence for education in Nigerian culture translates into a potent tool for success in the U.S.

Academic Excellence: Given the premium placed on education; many Nigerian immigrants pursue higher degrees. This academic inclination often results in them securing prestigious roles in various sectors, from medicine and law to academia and technology.

Holistic Development: The Nigerian perspective on education goes beyond academics. The emphasis on moral education and character development equips immigrants with integrity, diligence, and a strong work ethic – attributes highly valued in the professional world of the U.S.

The Synergistic Effect:

The interplay between these values creates a synergistic effect. The strong foundation of the family gives Nigerian immigrants the confidence to venture out, the community provides a safety net and a network, and the focus on education equips them with the skills to excel.

The success stories of Nigerian immigrants in the United States, while diverse in their details, echo a shared underlying theme – the indomitable strength derived from their cultural values. In the face of challenges that come with immigration – from adapting to a new culture to navigating socio-economic dynamics – the principles of family, community, and education offer Nigerian immigrants a blueprint for success. It's a testament to the idea that while our surroundings might change, the core values we carry can light our path, no matter where we are.

Chimamanda Ngozi Adichie: A Beacon of Nigerian Resilience and Excellence

In the realm of modern literature, few names resonate as profoundly as Chimamanda Ngozi

Adichie. With her eloquent prose, sharp insights, and the authenticity with which she captures the human experience, Adichie has carved a unique space for herself, not just as an author but as a bridge between cultures, continents, and generations. While her talents are undeniable, the roots of her success trace back to her Nigerian upbringing, which instilled in her the values of hard work, education, and family.

The Genesis: A Nigerian Household

Born in Enugu, Nigeria, Adichie's early years were steeped in an environment that cherished learning. Her father was a university professor, and her mother a university administrator - setting the stage for an environment where books were cherished companions and discussions, a daily ritual. The Nigerian reverence for education was not just an abstract concept for Adichie; it was a lived experience.

Education as a Compass: For Adichie, education was more than just formal schooling. It was about understanding the world, engaging with it, and finding one's voice. This holistic view of education, deeply ingrained in Nigerian culture, formed the cornerstone of her worldview. It propelled her to pursue studies in the United States, earning degrees from Eastern Connecticut State University, Johns Hopkins University, and Yale University.

Hard Work and Tenacity: The journey wasn't always smooth. Adichie navigated the complexities of being an African in America, often confronting stereotypes and biases. Yet, the Nigerian spirit of resilience, the belief that hard work can surmount challenges, saw her through. Her early rejections in the literary world did not deter her; they fueled her.

Family: The Unwavering Pillar

In several interviews, Adichie has often credited her family as a source of strength and inspiration. This doesn't merely allude to financial or logistical support but to a deeper, more intrinsic form of backing.

Stories from Home: Adichie's family narratives, tales of their Igbo heritage, the Biafran war, and the myriad complexities of Nigerian society, offered her a treasure trove of stories. Her novel, "Half of a Yellow Sun," which won the Orange Prize for Fiction, draws heavily from the history of the Biafran war, a story that was personal because of her family's experiences.

Moral and Ethical Grounding: Beyond tales, her family also instilled in her a strong moral compass. Adichie's works often grapple with heavy themes – identity, feminism, and post-colonialism. Her confident navigation through these themes can be attributed to the ethical grounding her family provided.

Bridging Cultures: A Unique Perspective

Adichie's position as a Nigerian-American gave her a unique vantage point. She could dissect the intricacies of both cultures, often juxtaposing them, leading to profound insights.

Challenging Stereotypes: In her famous TED Talk, "The Danger of a Single Story," Adichie delves into the reductive nature of cultural stereotypes. Her Nigerian upbringing, which taught her the value of diverse narratives and perspectives, became the foundation for this global message.

Feminism and Identity: Adichie' 's Nigerian background also influenced her views on feminism. In a society where gender roles are deeply entrenched, she learned the importance of challenging norms and asserting one's identity. Her book, "We Should All Be Feminists," is a testament to this belief, grounded in her Nigerian experiences but resonating globally.

Chapter 8: Social Networks

The Centrality of Social Networks in Nigerian Culture

Nigeria often termed the "Giant of Africa" due to its immense population and economic prowess, boasts a rich tapestry of cultures, ethnicities, and traditions. Stretching from the sprawling metropolis of Lagos to the arid landscapes of the Sahel in the north, from the oil-rich Niger Delta to the ancient city walls of Kano, the sheer diversity of this nation is awe-inspiring. Despite this multifaceted nature, there's a singular thread that binds the Nigerian fabric together: the vital role of social networks.

In Nigerian culture, social networks are more than just a set of relationships or connections. They represent trust, reciprocity, history, and sometimes even survival. These networks often extend beyond immediate families, encompassing extended kin, community members, old schoolmates, and even affiliations with ethnic or religious groups. The interconnectedness of these networks is what has, over centuries, enabled communities to thrive, individuals to find opportunities, and societies to maintain order.

A Historical Perspective

The importance of social networks in Nigeria is deep-rooted in history. Traditional societies relied on kinship networks for various functions, from trade to marriage negotiations, from settling disputes to seeking protection. Take, for instance, the age-old 'ajo' or 'Jesus' system. This indigenous form of cooperative banking involves a group of individuals contributing a fixed amount periodically and taking turns to collect the bulk sum. It's a practice that not only encourages thrift but underscores the significance of mutual trust and shared responsibility.

Beyond Economic Transactions

While the economic implications of such networks are evident, their societal value runs much deeper. In many Nigerian communities, one's reputation is intricately linked to one's family and network. The age-old saying, "It takes a village to raise a child," is lived daily in many parts of Nigeria. Children are often raised in communal settings and watched over by neighbors, relatives, and friends. This shared responsibility has fostered a strong sense of community and interdependence, with the welfare of the individual tightly knit with that of the group.

Social networks in Nigeria also play a pivotal role in the rites of passage – births, marriages, and deaths. These occasions are rarely private affairs. For example, traditional Nigerian weddings are grand spectacles, a testament to the couple's intertwined networks coming together. They symbolize not just the union of two individuals but the fusion of two families, sometimes even communities.

Social Networks in Modern Times

With the digital revolution, the dynamics of social networks in Nigeria have evolved, yet their essence remains unchanged. Platforms like Facebook, Twitter, and WhatsApp have become the virtual extensions of these real-world networks. They've enabled the Nigerian diaspora to remain connected, not just with family, but with their roots, traditions, and cultures.

However, it's essential to note that while digital platforms have amplified the reach of these networks, they haven't replaced the traditional modes. Instead, they've provided an additional layer, enabling greater connectivity and reinforcing age-old bonds. For instance, crowdfunding campaigns for community projects or medical emergencies often gain traction on social media, mobilizing not only close friends and family but also distant acquaintances and strangers bound by shared cultural or regional identities.

Challenges and Opportunities

Like all systems, social networks in Nigeria come with their challenges. Expectations from one's network can sometimes be overbearing, leading to societal pressures and a sense of obligation. Moreover, in a country grappling with issues of ethnic and religious divides, these networks, if narrowly defined, can perpetuate stereotypes or foster divisions.

Yet, the potential of these networks as catalysts for positive change is undeniable. Leveraging these vast and intricate webs of relationships can be the key to addressing some of Nigeria's pressing challenges, from entrepreneurial ventures to grassroots social initiatives.

In understanding Nigeria – its pulse, its challenges, and its opportunities – one cannot overlook the profound significance of its social networks. They are the lifeblood of its communities, the pillars of its societal structures, and the bridges to its future. As Nigeria continues to evolve in a rapidly globalizing world, these networks will undoubtedly play a crucial role in shaping the nation's destiny.

From Homeland to New Horizons: The Power of Social Networks

When Nigerians emigrate, they often carry more than just their suitcases. They bring their cultures, values, memories, and, most importantly, their innate sense of community. For Nigerian immigrants, social networks aren't just about staying connected; they're lifelines in unfamiliar terrains, instrumental in supporting each other and scaling the ladders of success.

Starting With a Helping Hand

The journey of a Nigerian immigrant, like many others, begins with a myriad of challenges - securing housing, understanding the local bureaucracy, finding employment, and, sometimes, simply navigating a new public transportation system. Here, the already-established social networks play a pivotal role. Before even setting foot in a new country, many Nigerian immigrants have a contact, be it a distant relative, a friend, or a friend of a friend, who can offer initial guidance. This person often acts as the first anchor, easing the transition into a foreign environment.

The Shared Knowledge Repository

Nigerian immigrant communities frequently come together to share insights, ranging from job opportunities to navigating local customs.

These networks act as unofficial "knowledge banks." For instance, understanding the nuances of a foreign job market can be daunting. But within these networks, there's likely someone who's been through the same process, ready to offer insights, tips, or even referrals.

The same applies to academic pursuits. Senior students often mentor newcomers, guiding them through admission processes, scholarship applications, and other academic challenges. This shared knowledge repository ensures that individual experiences benefit the entire community.

Cultural and Emotional Anchors

In the face of homesickness or cultural shock, these networks serve as emotional support systems. They're spaces where immigrants can celebrate familiar festivals, enjoy native cuisines, or simply converse in their local dialects. The shared experience of migration and the mutual longing for home create deep bonds, ensuring that members of the community can lean on each other during tough times.

Economic Empowerment

Nigerians abroad have earned a reputation for their entrepreneurial spirit. Often, their initial ventures are backed, both financially and morally, by their social networks. From Nigerian restaurants to export-import businesses dealing in native goods, these entrepreneurial endeavors frequently find their first customers, promoters, and even investors within the community. As they grow, they not only provide services to the diaspora but also create employment opportunities, further aiding new immigrants.

Challenges and The Way Forward

While these social networks offer a plethora of advantages, they also come with potential pitfalls. There's the risk of insularity, where immigrants remain within the confines of their community, limiting interactions with the broader populace. This can sometimes slow down the integration process.

However, with the advent of technology and the globalized nature of today's world, many Nigerian immigrant communities are actively bridging this gap. Digital platforms enable them to expand their networks, integrating with other communities while maintaining their unique identity.

The story of Nigerian immigrants isn't just about individual success stories; it's about collective resilience, mutual support, and the power of community. Their social networks are a testament to the age-old African proverb: "If you want to go fast, go alone. If you want to go far, go together." In the face of challenges, these networks have ensured that Nigerian immigrants don't just survive in new lands; they thrive, contribute, and shine.

Social Networks and the Nigerian Immigrant Success

Migration, in its very essence, is a leap into the unknown. But for many Nigerian immigrants, this leap is cushioned and directed by robust social networks. From the bustling streets of Lagos to the towering skyscrapers of New York, the journey of many a Nigerian has been bolstered by connections, community, and a collective spirit. This chapter delves into the inspiring tales of those who've harnessed the power of their networks to forge paths of success in foreign lands.

Business ventures flourishing from community bonds

Take the story of Chinedu, who arrived in London with dreams of introducing authentic Nigerian flavors to the British palate. With limited capital but a treasure trove of family recipes, he initially struggled to find the right market. But it was his Nigerian network in the city – a combination of old schoolmates, extended family, and connections made through local Nigerian associations – that gave him his first break. They not only became his first customers but also his most vocal promoters. Today, Chinedu runs a chain of successful Nigerian restaurants across the UK, a testament to the potential of community-driven entrepreneurship.

Or consider Ada, who leveraged her network to launch a fashion line inspired by traditional Nigerian fabrics. Her community not only provided initial seed funding but also helped connect her with local artisans in Nigeria. What started as a small venture catering to the

Nigerian diaspora soon garnered widespread appeal, showcasing the rich tapestry of Nigerian culture to the world.

Job Opportunities through Extended Networks

For many immigrants, the first and most pressing challenge is employment. Here, too, the power of the Nigerian network shines through. Tolu, an engineer, moved to Canada with stellar qualifications but little knowledge of the local job market. Through a church group, he connected with fellow Nigerians who had been in the country for longer. It was through these interactions that he learned about industry-specific job portals, fine-tuned his applications based on local preferences, and eventually landed a role in a leading tech firm.

Across the world, countless such stories abound – of Nigerians finding opportunities, not just through formal channels, but via a network that understands their journey, shares their aspirations, and is invested in their success.

Navigating Immigration Challenges

Immigration processes, with their complex web of regulations, documentation, and ever-changing policies, can be a daunting hurdle. But many Nigerians have successfully navigated this maze, thanks to insights and support from their networks.

Fatima, for instance, was on the brink of losing her visa status in the U. S. due to an administrative oversight. Unfamiliar with the intricacies of the system and unable to afford legal counsel, she turned to a local Nigerian association. Fellow community members connected her with Nigerian legal professionals in the area who offered pro bono advice. Not only did she manage to resolve her visa issue, but she also later became an advocate, helping others in similar predicaments.

The narratives of Nigerian immigrants underscore a universal truth: success isn't just born out of individual grit or talent but is often sculpted through collective effort. The successes of Nigerian immigrants in various fields – business, employment, and navigating the labyrinth of immigration – aren't just their successes; they're triumphs of a community, of connections that span continents, and of the undying Nigerian spirit that believes in lifting as it climbs.

John Dabiri: A Pioneer in Unsteady Fluid Mechanics and Biological Propulsion

John Oluseun Dabiri, a Nigerian-American aeronautics engineer, has established himself as a luminary in the field of unsteady fluid mechanics and biological propulsion. Holding the prestigious title of the Centennial Chair

Professor at the California Institute of Technology (Caltech), Dabiri has made significant contributions through his roles in the Graduate Aerospace Laboratories (GALCIT) and Mechanical Engineering departments. As the Director of the Biological Propulsion Laboratory, he spearheads research that spans aquatic locomotion, fluid dynamic energy conversion, and cardiac flows, employing theoretical methods in fluid dynamics and exploring the principles of optimal vortex formation.

Early Life: A Foundation Built on Curiosity and Inspiration

Born in Toledo, Ohio, Dabiri's early interest in science and engineering was kindled by the influence of his father, an engineer, and his mother, a science teacher. This interest led him to the University of Michigan, where he pursued a degree in mechanical engineering. It was here that his passion for fluid mechanics took root, inspired by research experiences that unveiled the complex behaviors of fluids.

Academic Pursuits: Exploring the Intricacies of Fluid Dynamics

After graduating with honors, Dabiri advanced to Princeton University for his Ph.D. in mechanical and aerospace engineering. Under the mentorship of Morteza Gharib, a leading fluid dynamicist, Dabiri explored the realms of biological propulsion, examining how various organisms utilize fluid dynamics for efficient locomotion.

Research Breakthroughs: Revolutionizing Biological Propulsion

Dabiri's doctoral work, focusing on the hydrodynamics of swimming and flying animals, led to groundbreaking insights in biological propulsion. His research revealed that these organisms employ optimal vortex formation to achieve efficient propulsion, a discovery that has significantly impacted biomechanics, aerospace engineering, and robotics. His findings have paved the way for bio-inspired propulsion systems in diverse applications, from underwater vehicles and aerial robots to medical devices.

Entrepreneurial Ventures: From Academia to Industry

Dabiri's innovative spirit transcends academic research. He co-founded Fluidic Energy and Fish Vortex Technologies, companies that capitalize on bio-inspired propulsion technologies. Fluidic Energy is focused on developing high-efficiency industrial pumps, while Fish Vortex Technologies is dedicated to designing energy-efficient underwater vehicles.

Awards and Recognition: A Testament to Excellence

Dabiri's remarkable contributions to science and engineering have been recognized with several prestigious awards, including:

- The Alan T. Waterman Award (2006)

- A MacArthur Fellowship (2006)

- The G. Evelyn Hutchinson Award (2011)

- Membership in the National Academy of Engineering (2017)

Legacy and Global Impact

John Dabiri's work stands as a testament to the power of interdisciplinary research in addressing complex global challenges. His pioneering research in unsteady fluid mechanics and biological propulsion has not only deepened our understanding of natural phenomena but also catalysed the development of cutting-edge technologies with wide-ranging applications.

Dabiri continues to be an inspirational figure for aspiring scientists and engineers, demonstrating the profound impact of curiosity-driven research and the importance of bridging theoretical knowledge with practical innovation. As he forges ahead in his quest to harness the power of fluids, his legacy continues to grow, shaping the future of science and engineering.

Chapter 9: Religion

Nigeria, often referred to as the "Giant of Africa," pulsates with a rich tapestry of cultures, languages, and histories. Amidst this vibrant mosaic, religion stands as a profound pillar, shaping identities, narratives, and the very ethos of Nigerian society. This chapter delves deep into the role of religion in Nigerian culture, tracing its influences, manifestations, and its pivotal role in weaving the diverse threads of the nation into a cohesive tapestry.

The Multifaceted Landscape of Nigerian Religion

Nigeria's religious landscape is as diverse as its people. Predominantly, three major religions coexist: Christianity, Islam, and traditional African religions. Christianity is primarily practiced in the southern and central regions, Islam in the northern and southwestern regions, and indigenous religions are interspersed throughout, though their prevalence has waned in the face of the Abrahamic religions.

Christianity: Brought to the shores of Nigeria by European missionaries in the 15th century, Christianity has grown to be a major force, with denominations ranging from Roman Catholicism to Anglican, Pentecostal, and Evangelical churches. These churches are not just places of worship but are integral community hubs, providing education, healthcare, and social services.

Islam: With roots tracing back to the 11th century through trans-Saharan trade and the influence of the Kanem-Borno Empire, Islam is deeply embedded in the culture of many northern Nigerians. Apart from the spiritual dimensions, Islam in Nigeria plays a role in the educational system, especially with Quranic schools (Almajiri) and the application of Sharia law in several northern states.

Traditional Religions: Before the advent and proliferation of Christianity and Islam, Nigerians practiced a plethora of indigenous religions. Although many of these practices have been overshadowed, they remain influential, especially in rituals, festivals, and the arts. Deities like Sango (god of thunder) and Olokun (god of the sea) are celebrated and revered in various parts of the country.

Religion as Identity and Community

In Nigeria, religion is more than just a spiritual pursuit; it's an identity. From names to dressing styles, dietary choices to life ceremonies, religious beliefs deeply influence the everyday lives of Nigerians. Moreover, religious gatherings, whether Friday Jumu'ah prayers, Sunday masses, or traditional festivals, serve as communal focal points, fostering unity, shared values, and social cohesion.

The Interplay of Religion and Politics

Religion and politics in Nigeria are deeply intertwined. From the formation of political alliances to policy decisions and the enactment of laws, religious considerations often come to the forefront. While this interplay has been a source of solidarity for many, it has also led to tensions, particularly in regions with religious diversity.

Arts, Music, and Literature: The Religious Imprint

Nigeria's rich artistic heritage, from its literature to music and dance, is steeped in religious influences. Gospel music thrives alongside Islamic Nasheeds, while traditional festivals like the Osun Osogbo celebrate ancient deities with fervor. Writers like Chinua Achebe and Wole Soyinka have woven religious motifs into their works, reflecting the intricate blend of the spiritual and the mundane in Nigerian life.

Challenges and the Path Forward

While religion offers solace, identity, and community to millions, it has also been a source of strife. Inter-religious tensions, particularly between Christian and Muslim communities, have occasionally erupted, demanding introspection and dialogue. As Nigeria strides forward, the call is for a pluralistic understanding where diverse religious beliefs coexist harmoniously, enriching the nation's fabric.

Religion in Nigeria is a pulsating beat, echoing the hopes, histories, and aspirations of its people. From the call to prayer resonating from minarets in Kano to the harmonious hymns in Calabar churches and the rhythmic dances in honor of Yoruba deities, religion is an inextricable thread in the Nigerian narrative. It's a testament to Nigeria's rich legacy and its ability to harmonize diverse beliefs into a symphony of coexistence and shared destiny.

How Nigerian Immigrants Lean on Religion

The journey of an immigrant is seldom smooth. It's a patchwork of hope and uncertainty, ambition and nostalgia, new possibilities and lingering ties to the past. For Nigerian immigrants, these complexities are often navigated with an enduring ally: their religious beliefs. Faith, deeply embedded in the Nigerian ethos, remains a potent force in the diasporic journey, offering solace in challenging times and propelling individuals towards their dreams. This chapter delves into the pivotal role religion plays in the lives of Nigerian immigrants, cushioning blows and illuminating paths.

Faith as a Solace in Alien Lands

Upon setting foot in unfamiliar territories, many Nigerian immigrants confront a myriad of challenges: cultural shocks, racial prejudices, and the arduous task of establishing a new life. Here, religion emerges as a sanctuary. The familiarity of prayers, hymns, or rituals provides an emotional anchor, reconnecting them with their roots and offering solace amidst the chaos.

For instance, attending church services or mosque prayers not only becomes a spiritual exercise but also a space to reconnect with a semblance of home. It's where they hear familiar languages, share stories from back home, and find a community that understands their journey.

Religious Communities: A Network of Support

Beyond personal solace, religious institutions in the diaspora often evolve into robust support systems. Nigerian churches or mosques abroad frequently facilitate social services, from helping newcomers find accommodation and employment to guiding them through bureaucratic processes. The church or mosque isn't just a place of worship; it's a hub of communal activity, providing both spiritual and material sustenance.

For example, when Chijioke arrived in Canada, it was members of his local Nigerian church who helped him find his first job, navigate the city, and adjust to the biting cold. This tangible support, rooted in shared faith, eased his transition into a new world.

Religion as a Moral Compass and Motivator

The teachings and values imbibed from religious beliefs often serve as a moral compass, guiding Nigerian immigrants in their decisions and actions. Principles of integrity, perseverance, community service, and gratitude, frequently emphasized in religious texts, motivate many to pursue their goals with tenacity and ethics.

Consider Fatimah, a Nigerian immigrant pursuing medical studies in the UK. During her most challenging times, it was her Islamic faith that reminded her of the importance of patience, resilience, and the belief that challenges are tests designed for growth. Such convictions, stemming from her religious beliefs, fueled her determination to succeed.

Faith-inspired Entrepreneurial Ventures

Many Nigerian immigrants have also channeled their religious beliefs into entrepreneurial ventures, addressing the needs of their diasporic community. From opening Christian bookstores or Halal restaurants to launching apps that notify prayer times, faith becomes an avenue for innovation and business, serving both spiritual and practical needs.

A noteworthy example is Ngozi, who started a fashion line in the U.S., blending modern styles with modesty principles rooted in her Christian faith. Her brand resonated with many, leading to a successful enterprise that bridged faith and fashion.

Dealing with Adversity: The Power of Prayer and Community

When faced with life's adversities, from health challenges to financial setbacks, many Nigerian immigrants turn to prayer and their religious communities for strength. Believing in a higher power that oversees their journey offers comfort and perspective, reminding them that struggles are transient.

Moreover, communal prayer sessions or religious gatherings amplify this strength. The collective energy shared empathy, and communal prayers act as powerful reaffirmations of hope and resilience.

Nigerian Immigrants Rising Above Adversity

Faith often serves as the unseen bedrock upon which many immigrants build their aspirations and tackle the challenges of life in a new land. For Nigerian immigrants, whose rich cultural landscape is deeply intertwined with religion, faith often becomes the compass, directing their path and illuminating possibilities. In this chapter, we delve into the narratives of Nigerian immigrants who, fueled by their religious convictions, have transcended adversity to etch remarkable success stories.

Aisha's Odyssey: From Refugee to Renowned Physician

Aisha's journey from Nigeria to the shores of Europe wasn't a pursuit of dreams but an escape from nightmares. Fleeing religious conflict in her hometown, she found herself in a refugee camp, grappling with trauma and an uncertain future. Yet, her Islamic faith became her anchor. Drawing strength from the teachings of endurance and resilience in the Quran, Aisha pursued her passion for medicine. Fast forward a decade, and she stands tall as a renowned cardiologist, attributing her success to her unwavering faith that assured her brighter days lay ahead.

Emeka's Leap of Faith: A Business Empire Rooted in Belief

Arriving in Canada with limited funds and a pocketful of dreams, Emeka was determined to carve a niche for himself. Inspired by Biblical teachings on hard work and providence, he initiated a small venture importing Nigerian food items. Trusting in his Christian principles of integrity and service, his business expanded exponentially. Today, Emeka's chain of stores not only offers Nigerians abroad a taste of home but also employs hundreds, turning a leap of faith into a tangible legacy.

Chinasa's Dance: Preserving Culture through Faith-Inspired Arts

Chinasa's move to the U.S. was accompanied by a fervent desire to preserve her Nigerian heritage. Drawing from her indigenous religious beliefs and practices, she founded a dance academy that blended traditional Nigerian dance forms with spiritual narratives. The academy grew, fostering cultural preservation and creating a bridge between generations. For Chinasa, dance wasn't just an art; it was a prayer, an expression of gratitude to the deities she believed had guided her path.

Tunde's Mission: A Tech Innovator Inspired by Service

Tunde's journey from Lagos to Silicon Valley was marked by numerous challenges, from racial biases to the cut-throat competition of the tech world. But his Islamic faith, with its emphasis on community service and perseverance, became his guiding light. Tunde developed apps tailored to the needs of Muslim communities abroad, from Halal restaurant finders to platforms facilitating charitable donations. His ventures, rooted in faith-driven service, not only brought him professional success but also enriched the lives of countless individuals.

Joy's Sanctuary: Turning Trauma into Healing

Joy's transition to life in the UK was marred by personal adversities, from battling mental health issues to grappling with the loss of loved ones back home. Yet, her Christian faith, with its promise of redemption and hope, propelled her forward. Drawing from her experiences and her belief in the healing power of faith, Joy established a counseling center catering specifically to the emotional needs of immigrants. Her center, a sanctuary of healing, became a testament to the transformative power of faith in the face of adversity.

The tales of Aisha, Emeka, Chinasa, Tunde, and Joy are but a few drops in the vast ocean of narratives where faith has played a pivotal role in shaping the destinies of Nigerian immigrants. While their journeys are distinct, a common thread binds them: an unwavering faith that transformed challenges into opportunities, despair into hope, and dreams into realities.

 For these individuals, religion wasn't a passive aspect of their identity; it was an active force guiding their decisions, fueling their aspirations, and grounding them in times of turmoil. Their stories underscore the profound impact of religious beliefs in navigating the intricacies of the immigrant experience.

In the face of adversities that often seemed insurmountable, their faith reminded them of their strength, their purpose, and the promise of a brighter tomorrow. Through their triumphs, they not only etched personal success stories but also illuminated the path for countless others, showcasing the enduring power of faith in the diasporic journey.

Slam Dunk with Faith: The Hakeem Olajuwon Story

In the sprawling arena of basketball legends, certain names resonate not only for their impeccable skills on the court but for their deep-rooted values that transcend the game. Hakeem Olajuwon, a towering figure both in stature and legacy, is one such name. A Nigerian-American who dominated the basketball courts of the NBA, Olajuwon's journey was as much about faith as it was about slam dunks. This chapter delves into how Olajuwon's Muslim faith shaped his basketball journey, providing focus, motivation, and a moral compass that steered him to greatness.

From Lagos to Houston: The Rise of a Basketball Phenom

Hakeem's journey from the bustling streets of Lagos to the illuminated courts of the NBA wasn't just a testament to his athletic prowess but also a reflection of his indomitable spirit fueled by his faith. Emigrating from Nigeria to the United States, Olajuwon faced the usual challenges of an immigrant: cultural adjustments, homesickness, and the pressures of fitting in. Yet, as the challenges grew, so did his reliance on his Muslim faith.

Faith on the Court: Islam as Hakeem's Guiding Force

The basketball court is a mélange of speed, strategy, and skill. Amidst the cacophony of roaring fans and aggressive plays, Olajuwon found his calm by grounding himself in his faith. The principles of Islam, with its emphasis on discipline, humility, and dedication, resonated deeply with him. These principles became the foundation of his game.

During the rigorous training sessions, when exhaustion threatened to overwhelm them, it was his faith that kept him going. He often cited the discipline of daily prayers (Salat) in Islam as a regimen that helped him cultivate focus, patience, and resilience — qualities that became invaluable on the court.

Ramadan and the Playoffs: A Testament to Dedication

One of the most poignant moments showcasing the intersection of Hakeem's faith and his career was during the NBA playoffs, which coincided with the holy month of Ramadan. Observing fasts from dawn to dusk, Olajuwon's commitment to his faith was unwavering, even in the face of physically demanding matches.

Many were awestruck by his ability to deliver exceptional performances, all while fasting. For Hakeem, it wasn't about proving a point; it was simply a reflection of his deep-rooted belief that his strength and endurance stemmed from his faith.

The Role Model: Impact Beyond the Court

Olajuwon's success wasn't limited to his championships and awards. His journey as a devout Muslim in the high-octane world of professional basketball made him a role model for countless young athletes, particularly those from Muslim backgrounds. His story became a beacon of hope, illustrating that one need not compromise one's religious beliefs to achieve success.

He often spoke about the moral compass Islam provided him, guiding his actions on and off the court. From treating opponents with respect to engaging in charitable endeavors, Hakeem's life was a tapestry of lessons rooted in his faith.

Legacy and Beyond

Hakeem Olajuwon's story is not just about a basketball legend; it's about a man whose faith was his anchor, guiding him through the storms and sunshine of his career. In moments of victory, his faith kept him humble, and in moments of defeat, it kept him hopeful.

Today, as he imparts basketball skills to young aspirants, Olajuwon also shares the wisdom derived from his faith. His legacy, beautifully intertwined with the teachings of Islam, continues to inspire and motivate.

Hakeem Olajuwon's illustrious basketball journey serves as a powerful testament to the potent combination of talent, dedication, and unwavering faith. His story reminds us that true greatness is not just about accolades and achievements; it's about the values we uphold and the principles that guide our journey. In the annals of basketball history, Olajuwon will always be remembered not just for his unmatched skills but for the deep-seated faith that was the cornerstone of his success.

Chapter 10: Dreams and Goals

To Dream and To Dare: The Pillars of Nigerian Culture

Nigeria, often referred to as the 'Giant of Africa,' boasts a cultural tapestry woven from diverse ethnic groups, languages, and traditions. Yet, despite its multiplicity, a singular, unifying trait courses through the Nigerian psyche – an inherent ability to dream big and set ambitious goals. In this chapter, we delve deep into the cultural, historical, and societal facets of Nigeria that underscore the importance of dreams and goals, making them intrinsic components of its ethos.

Historical Backdrop: Rising from Adversity

Historically, Nigeria has weathered tumultuous storms – from the eras of slave trade and colonization to its struggle for independence and the subsequent socio-political challenges. Through each phase, the Nigerian spirit remained undaunted, with dreams and goals serving as the lighthouses guiding its path. It wasn't merely about survival; it was about shaping a destiny that future generations could be proud of.

Dreams in Folktales and Oral Traditions

The significance of dreams and aspirations is deeply embedded in Nigeria's oral traditions and folktales. Legends of heroes and heroines, often regaled to young listeners around communal fires, underscore the themes of ambition, resilience, and perseverance. These tales, passed down through generations, reinforce the idea that dreams are the seeds from which towering trees of success grow.

Cultural Celebrations: A Testament to Aspirations

Nigerian festivals, be it the colorful Durbar Festival of the north or the vibrant masquerades of the Igbo culture, are not just celebrations of tradition but also manifestations of communal dreams and goals. These festivals often represent the aspirations of entire communities, celebrating past achievements and setting the stage for future ambitions.

Modern Day Nigeria: Nollywood and Beyond

In contemporary Nigeria, the significance of dreams is most palpably felt in its booming entertainment industry. Nollywood, Nigeria's film industry, stands as a testament to what dreams can achieve. From humble beginnings, it has risen to become the world's second-largest film industry by volume. Behind every movie lies the dreams of writers, directors, actors, and countless others, all converging to tell a tale.

Similarly, the Nigerian music scene, producing global icons, underscores the nation's ability to dream beyond borders, setting goals that traverse continents.

Education and Dreams: The Nigerian Pursuit

In Nigerian households, education is often viewed as the golden key that unlocks doors to brighter futures. Parents dream of their children scaling academic heights, often making enormous sacrifices to ensure quality education. It's not merely about acquiring degrees; it's about equipping the next generation with tools to realize their own dreams.

Societal Structures and Goal Setting

The importance of setting clear goals is ingrained in various societal structures in Nigeria. From the traditional age-grade systems, where individuals within age brackets work collectively towards communal projects, to the urban entrepreneurship hubs fostering start-ups, the Nigerian landscape is dotted with goal-oriented endeavors.

Dreams and goals in Nigerian culture are not abstract concepts relegated to the realm of thought; they are tangible forces that shape actions, drive progress, and mold destinies. Whether it's the farmer in the hinterlands of Sokoto dreaming of a bounteous harvest or the tech entrepreneur in Lagos setting goals to break into the global market, the Nigerian spirit, ambitious and indomitable, remains ever fervent.

In the global narrative, Nigeria often emerges as a beacon of hope, showcasing that when dreams are backed by determination and goals are pursued with tenacity, milestones become mere stepping stones to greater glory. In the heart of Nigeria lies the profound belief that to dream is to hope, and to set goals is to affirm the promise of a brighter tomorrow.

A Diasporic Vision: Dreams and Goals Fueling Nigerian Immigrants' Success

The tale of immigration, no matter where it unfolds, is often one punctuated by challenges, nostalgia, and the pursuit of a better life. For Nigerian immigrants, this tale takes on a unique hue, deeply colored by their inherent ability to dream big and set transformative goals. The Nigerian spirit, resilient and ambitious, does not wane beyond its borders; it only intensifies, using dreams as its compass and goals as its roadmap. This chapter delves into how Nigerian immigrants harness their aspirations to carve success stories in foreign lands.

From Homeland to Foreign Shores: The Dream Takes Flight

The decision to immigrate, for many Nigerians, is not a mere change of geographical location; it's a dream-taking flight. Whether it's the pursuit of higher education in elite global institutions, tapping into better job opportunities, or simply seeking a life less encumbered by socio-political challenges, the underlying motif remains the same: the aspiration for an enhanced life.

Dreams as Resilience Tools

Navigating life in a foreign country comes with its own set of complexities. From cultural adjustments and battling stereotypes to overcoming economic challenges, the journey is fraught with hurdles. Yet, for many Nigerian immigrants, their dreams serve as reservoirs of resilience. When faced with adversity, they often draw from their deep wells of aspirations, using them as buffers against despair and pathways to perseverance.

Goal-Setting: A Bridge to Integration

Setting clear, tangible goals has often aided Nigerian immigrants in their integration journey.

Whether it's mastering a new language, acquiring qualifications that align with their career ambitions in the new country, or even establishing community organizations that foster connections, these goals become bridges, aiding them in building their lives in unfamiliar terrains.

Success Stories: Dreams Manifested

The global diaspora is dotted with Nigerian immigrants who have turned their dreams into tangible realities:

I. In academia, Nigerian scholars, driven by their goal to contribute to global knowledge, often emerge as thought leaders in their respective fields.

II. In the arts, Nigerian writers, musicians, and filmmakers, fueled by their dreams of showcasing their heritage, have garnered international acclaim, with their works resonating across cultures.

III. The entrepreneurial world has seen numerous Nigerians, their dreams undeterred by the initial paucity of resources, establish ventures that not only thrive but also contribute significantly to their adopted countries' economies.

The Role of Community: Collective Dreaming

One cannot underscore enough the role of the Nigerian immigrant community in nurturing individual dreams. Often, these communities become incubators of aspirations. Shared experiences, collective problem-solving, and a deep sense of camaraderie ensure that when one dreams, the community rallies behind them, turning personal goals into collective endeavors.

The Legacy of Dreams: Forging Pathways for Future Generations

The success stories of Nigerian immigrants, powered by their dreams and goals, lay the groundwork for future generations. Their achievements, whether in academia, business, or community service, serve as blueprints, instilling in the younger generation the belief that dreams, no matter how lofty, are achievable.

Dreams and goals, for Nigerian immigrants, are not mere ephemeral concepts; they are the lifeblood of their diasporic journey. These aspirations, deeply rooted in their cultural ethos, become their North Star in foreign lands, guiding them through challenges, fueling their ambitions, and scripting success stories that inspire.

In a world that often seems fragmented, the tale of Nigerian immigrants stands as a testament to the unifying power of dreams. It reminds us that no matter where we hail from, our aspirations when pursued with fervor and focus, have the potential to transcend borders, break barriers, and illuminate the world with stories of hope, determination, and triumph.

The Nigerian Spirit Beyond Borders: Triumphs of Tenacity

Nigerian immigrants, a subset of the global diaspora, are often heralded for their unparalleled grit, resilience, and ambition. Their stories, woven with threads of challenges and victories, provide inspiration to countless others, reminding us that success is often the child of tenacity and unwavering focus. As we embark on this chapter, we shine the spotlight on Nigerian immigrants who, against all odds, transformed their dreams into tangible realities, leaving indelible imprints on the world.

The Foundation of Success: The Nigerian Ethos

Nigeria, with its rich cultural tapestry, has always been a cradle of dreams. Whether it's the folktales passed down through generations that emphasize triumphs over adversities or the communal celebrations that echo collective achievements, the narrative has consistently been one of ambition and perseverance. This cultural foundation becomes the bedrock for Nigerian immigrants as they chart their success stories in foreign lands.

Dreams Beyond Borders

For many Nigerian immigrants, the journey begins with a dream, often nurtured in the bustling streets of Lagos or the tranquil plains of Jos. However, what sets these dreams apart is the unyielding commitment to see them through. As they navigate unfamiliar terrains, battle stereotypes, and face economic challenges, their goals act as anchors, grounding them and propelling them forward.

Success Chronicles: The Nigerian Imprint

From literature and arts to politics and sciences, Nigerian immigrants have etched their names in golden letters:

1. **Literature:** Notable figures like Chimamanda Ngozi Adichie, with her poignant tales reflecting both her Nigerian heritage and global experiences, have dominated international literary scenes.

2. **Medicine:** Nigerian doctors, researchers, and healthcare professionals across the globe

have been at the forefront of medical innovations and services, driven by their goals to make a difference.

3. Technology: Silicon Valley and other tech hubs worldwide have witnessed the meteoric rise of Nigerian tech experts, entrepreneurs, and innovators who, with their groundbreaking ventures, have redefined the tech landscape.

Ndidi Nwuneli: A Nigerian-American Educator, Innovator, and Leader

Ndidi Nwuneli stands as a paragon of educational excellence and leadership, deeply rooted in her Nigerian-American heritage. Born on March 22, 1975, at the University of Nigeria Teaching Hospital in Enugu, Nigeria, to a Nigerian professor of Pharmacology, Paul Obuekwe Okonkwo, and an American professor of History, Rina Okonkwo, Nwuneli's life has been a blend of diverse cultural and academic influences. Her parents, both educators, instilled in her and her siblings the values of patriotism, service, and resilience, even amidst the challenging political climate of the late General Sani Abacha years in Nigeria.

Educational Prowess and Early Achievements

Nwuneli's educational journey is marked by notable accomplishments. By 1997, she was a student at Harvard Business School (HBS), where she earned both the Harvey Fellowship and the National Black MBA Association Graduate Scholarship, recognizing her academic excellence. Her extracurricular activities at Harvard included founding and co-chairing the Annual African Business Conference and serving in various leadership roles within the student community. She graduated with her MBA at the young age of 24 in 1999.

A Career Defined by Impact and Leadership

Ndidi Nwuneli's career began with a Summer Business Analyst position at McKinsey & Company in New York during her junior year at The University of Pennsylvania. This role evolved into a full-time position, where she worked in Chicago and Johannesburg, contributing significantly to projects that enhanced police training and reduced crime rates in South Africa.

Transformative Work in Nigeria

In 1999, Nwuneli took on a leadership role as the Lead Consultant for The Ford Foundation, focusing on Nigeria's largest microcredit institutions. She rejoined McKinsey, providing consultancy for consumer goods companies and large American retailers, before returning to Nigeria in 2000 to serve as the executive director for the FATE Foundation. Her work in Nigeria is characterized by a focus on empowering women entrepreneurs and addressing challenges in education and business growth.

Founding Nonprofits and Shaping Futures

In 2002, Nwuneli founded two nonprofits: LEAP Africa, focusing on youth leadership development, and Ndu Ike Akunuba (NIA), emphasizing female empowerment. Under her leadership, LEAP Africa has partnered with significant global organizations and foundations, contributing to youth leadership training programs.

Governance and Board Roles

Ndidi Nwuneli has held influential positions on various boards, including LEAP Africa, AACE Foods, Godrej Group, DSM Sustainability Advisory Board, AGRA, and Nigerian Breweries Plc. Her contributions extend to global platforms like the Rockefeller Foundation, the Nigerian Economic Summit Group, and Stanbic IBTC, showcasing her expertise and commitment to governance and sustainable development.

Vision for West Africa's Agricultural Transformation

One of Nwuneli's key goals is transforming West Africa's agricultural landscape, envisioning the sector as the region's "new gold." Her work in this area is aimed at building a robust ecosystem that supports sustainable agriculture and economic growth.

A Legacy of Education, Innovation, and Leadership

Ndidi Nwuneli's journey is a testament to the power of education, the impact of visionary leadership, and the importance of cultural integration. Her achievements in various sectors, from business consultancy to nonprofit management, reflect her commitment to empowering others, particularly in the realms of youth leadership and women's entrepreneurship. Her legacy is one of inspiration, innovation, and unwavering dedication to improving lives and communities, both in Nigeria and beyond.

Chapter 11: Resilience

Bending but Unbreakable – The Resilience of the Nigerian Spirit

In the vast tapestry of human qualities, resilience emerges as one of the most formidable threads, a trait that enables individuals to navigate the stormiest waters and still find their way to shore. Within Nigerian culture, resilience is not just a trait – it's an ethos. Rooted deeply in their collective psyche, Nigerians, both at home and abroad, often draw from this well of resilience to turn adversities into opportunities. In this chapter, we delve deep into the essence of Nigerian resilience and the ways in which Nigerian immigrants harness it to script their success stories in foreign lands.

The Nigerian Legacy of Resilience

The history of Nigeria is a testament to the indomitable spirit of its people. From colonial struggles to internal conflicts, economic challenges, and societal upheavals, the nation has seen its fair share of trials. Yet, time and again, its people have risen, adapting, evolving, and pushing forward. This resilience is infused in their folklore, their music, their art, and their daily lives. It's an inherited legacy, passed down from one generation to the next, reminding them that while they may bend, they never break.

The Resilience of Immigrants: From Familiarity to Foreignness

Migration, in itself, is an act of resilience. Uprooting oneself from familiar terrains to venture into the unknown requires immense courage and adaptability. For Nigerian immigrants, this journey often comes with its unique set of challenges: cultural shocks, economic hardships, and, sometimes, battles against biases. However, what sets their narrative apart is their ability to use these very challenges as stepping stones, drawing strength from their inherent resilience.

Anchors of Resilience: Community and Heritage

One of the most significant pillars of resilience for Nigerian immigrants is their strong sense of community and their unwavering connection to their heritage. Whether it's community gatherings, religious congregations, or simply informal meet-ups, these interactions serve as safe spaces where they can draw strength, share their struggles, and collectively find solutions.

Their rich heritage, with its tales of triumphs over adversities, serves as a constant reminder of their lineage of resilience.

Scripting Success: Resilience in Action

Across the globe, Nigerian immigrants have emerged as leaders, innovators, academics, artists, and much more. Their success stories, while varied, have one common thread: resilience.

Academia: Many Nigerian scholars, faced with limited resources and opportunities in their homeland, have ventured abroad, navigating the challenging terrains of foreign education systems to emerge as thought leaders.

Entrepreneurship: The landscape is dotted with Nigerian immigrants who, starting with limited capital and facing myriad challenges, have built successful enterprises, contributing significantly to their adopted countries.

Arts: Nigerian artists, musicians, and writers have often used their craft to narrate their tales of resilience, creating masterpieces that resonate globally.

The Nigerian narrative, both at home and in the diaspora, is a testament to the power of resilience. It serves as a poignant reminder that challenges can be overcome with grit, determination, and an unwavering spirit, no matter how insurmountable they may seem. For Nigerian immigrants, resilience is not just an inherited trait; it's a chosen way of life. As they traverse foreign lands, build homes away from home, and script success stories, they shine a light on the indomitable Nigerian spirit – bending under pressure but never breaking, adapting to challenges but never losing their essence. Their journey underscores a universal truth: with resilience, the human spirit can survive adversities and thrive, turning trials into triumphs.

From Setbacks to Comebacks - The Unyielding Nigerian Spirit

Amidst the vast diaspora tales, stories of Nigerian immigrants stand out, not just for their success but for the often-Herculean challenges they surmount to achieve it. They teach us an essential life lesson: setbacks can be set up for comebacks if one holds on to one's dreams. In this chapter, we highlight the success of those Nigerian immigrants who, despite facing dire straits, never relinquished their dreams.

Facing Challenges Head-On: The Nigerian Immigrant's Journey

Migration is seldom easy. Moving from familiar terrains to the unfamiliar, coupled with the complexities of navigating new cultures, systems, and often prejudices, can be daunting. Nigerian immigrants often juggle these challenges along with personal adversities. Job losses, cultural shocks, financial crises - the list is exhaustive. Yet, their narratives frequently don't end in despair. Instead, they reshape these adversities, using them as catalysts to pursue their dreams with even more vigor.

The Will to Rise: Nigerian Immigrants' Success Stories

From academia to entrepreneurship, arts to sciences, Nigerian immigrants have showcased those dreams, when fueled by determination, can overcome any impediment:

Literature: Authors like Teju Cole and Chimamanda Ngozi Adichie have faced significant hurdles in their journeys but emerged as powerful voices, their works resonating globally.

Science & Tech: Despite initial struggles, many Nigerian immigrants have climbed the ladder in Silicon Valley, making a mark in the tech industry.

Entertainment: Artists like David Adeleke, popularly known as Davido, despite facing challenges, have made it big in international music arenas, showcasing the global appeal of Nigerian talent.

David Adedeji Adeleke: A Nigerian-American Singer, Songwriter, and Record Producer

David Adedeji Adeleke, globally recognized by his stage name Davido, stands as a towering figure in the music industry, embodying the vibrant synergy of Nigerian and American cultures. Born in Atlanta, Georgia, on November 21, 1992, to Nigerian parents, Davido's upbringing in both Nigeria and the United States laid the foundation for his unique musical style. His early inclination towards music quickly evolved into a flourishing career, marking him as a significant artist while still in college.

Musical Odyssey: From Early Beginnings to International Fame

Davido's journey to stardom commenced with his debut studio album, "Omo Baba Olowo" ("Son of a Rich Man"), in 2011. This album not only cemented his status in Nigeria but also set the stage for his international acclaim. His 2017 single "Fall" became a global sensation, topping charts across Africa, Europe, and North America, and earning him a Grammy Award nomination for Best African Pop/R&B Album. His discography expanded with hits like "If," "Aye," and "Gobe," showcasing collaborations with international stars such as Chris Brown, Nicki Minaj, and Major Lazer.

Entrepreneurship and Humanitarian Initiatives

Davido's talents extend beyond the music studio. He founded HKN Music, a record label instrumental in launching the careers of several Nigerian artists. His entrepreneurial spirit also led him to co-found the Aje Group, with investments spanning real estate, entertainment, and fashion.

His philanthropic contributions are equally noteworthy. The Davido Music Worldwide (DMW) Foundation, established by him, provides financial aid to orphans and the underprivileged. His involvement in various charitable initiatives, supporting education and healthcare, demonstrates his commitment to giving back to society.

Cultural Ambassador and Advocate

As a cultural icon, Davido has transcended the boundaries of music. He is a symbol of success and resilience for many young Africans, challenging global stereotypes about the African continent. His advocacy for African art and culture, coupled with his stance against racism and discrimination, has made him a prominent figure in promoting African heritage on a global stage.

Accolades and Awards

David Adeleke's impact in music and beyond has been recognized with a plethora of awards, including:

- BET Awards for Best International Act (2014, 2017)

- MTV Europe Music Awards for Best African Act (2015, 2017, 2021)

- Soul Train Music Awards for Best International Song (2017)

- Nigeria Entertainment Awards for Best Male Artist (2012-2016)

- The Headies for Artist of the Year (2012, 2014, 2017)

Legacy: A Fusion of Music, Entrepreneurship, and Philanthropy

Davido's legacy is multifaceted: a testament to his musical genius, entrepreneurial acumen, and philanthropic efforts. He stands as an inspiration, demonstrating that success is attainable irrespective of one's background. His music, characterized by its energy and cross-cultural appeal, continues to unite people worldwide, making him a pivotal figure in the global music scene.

Chapter 12: Optimism

The Radiant Horizon - The Power of Nigerian Optimism

The indomitable spirit of the Nigerian people, often marked by an unwavering sense of hope, resonates deeply within their cultural ethos. This pervasive optimism isn't merely a pleasant outlook but a powerful life force, enabling individuals to weather storms with grace, converting adversities into opportunities. In this chapter, we shine a spotlight on the centrality of optimism in Nigerian culture and its instrumental role in guiding Nigerian immigrants through the maze of challenges, ensuring they remain spirited and inspired.

The Roots of Optimism in Nigerian Culture

Nigeria, with its rich tapestry of ethnicities, languages, and traditions, is also a land of contrasts. From bustling cities to serene villages, modernity to tradition, prosperity to adversity, Nigeria's landscape is diverse. Through it all, one sentiment stands unwavering: optimism.

Historical narratives, folk tales, music, and even day-to-day interactions in Nigeria carry undertones of hope and a brighter tomorrow. Community gatherings often revolve around storytelling sessions where tales of hardship and eventual triumph, often against all odds, are shared and celebrated. This cultural predisposition towards optimism is a coping mechanism and a deeply ingrained way of life.

The Optimistic Immigrant: Hope Beyond Borders

Migration is inherently a venture of hope. While navigating the myriad challenges of resettlement - from cultural shifts and potential biases to economic uncertainties - Nigerian immigrants often deploy their innate optimism as a compass. This isn't a naive or unfounded optimism but a cultivated mindset that recognizes challenges and yet chooses to focus on potential silver linings.

1. Optimism as a Buffer: The initial days of immigration can be daunting. An unfamiliar environment, potential loneliness, and the struggle to establish oneself can be overwhelming. Here, optimism acts as a cushion, softening the blow of hardships and ensuring that one's spirit isn't easily broken.

2. Visionary Optimism: The ability to envision a better future, even when the present is clouded with difficulties, is a hallmark of Nigerian optimism. This visionary optimism allows immigrants to set ambitious goals and persevere toward them, undeterred by temporary setbacks.

3. Community and Collective Optimism: Nigerian immigrants often establish close-knit communities in their new homes, reiterating and reinforcing their optimistic outlook. Shared experiences, collective celebrations, and mutual encouragement amplify the sense of hope and provide the needed motivation.

Optimism, for Nigerians, isn't a mere emotion – it's a powerful tool, a guiding light. In the labyrinth of life, filled with unforeseen challenges and unexpected turns, this optimistic spirit acts as a beacon, ensuring they never lose their way. For Nigerian immigrants, optimism is both an inheritance from their homeland and a chosen weapon to carve their niche in foreign terrains.

In the words of a Nigerian proverb, "No matter how dark the night, dawn will surely come." This sentiment encapsulates the Nigerian essence – a belief that no matter how convoluted the journey, a brighter destination awaits. It's this radiant horizon, perpetually in sight, that keeps the Nigerian spirit buoyant and ever-hopeful.

The Bright Side - Optimism in the Nigerian Immigrant's Journey

Migration, in many ways, is an embodiment of optimism. The act of leaving familiar shores for uncharted territories comes with the inherent hope of better opportunities and a brighter future. For Nigerian immigrants, this optimism isn't merely an accessory they carry along with them; it's a lifeline. It serves as a beacon, guiding them through the dark tunnels of challenges, ensuring they emerge resilient and triumphant. In this chapter, we delve deeper into how this optimism defines the journey of Nigerian immigrants, helping them navigate obstacles with an undying spirit.

Optimism: The Invisible Armor

Immigrating to a new country often comes with its fair share of hurdles. The trials range from settling into unfamiliar cultural terrains, encountering potential biases, and grappling with homesickness to navigating economic uncertainties. It's during these trying times that the inherent optimism of Nigerian immigrants shines brightest.

1. Overcoming Cultural Differences: Immersing oneself in an entirely different culture can be daunting. But rather than viewing it as an obstacle, many Nigerian immigrants harness their optimism to perceive it as an enriching experience. This positive outlook helps them embrace diversity, learn from it, and even find parallels between their native and adopted cultures.

2. Tackling Economic Challenges: Financial hardships and the pressure to provide can weigh heavily on the immigrant's shoulders. However, fueled by optimism, many immigrants use these challenges as motivation.

They often work tirelessly, further their education, and seek better opportunities, believing fervently in the prospect of a brighter financial future.

3. Combatting Prejudices: Facing biases can be disheartening. Yet, the optimistic Nigerian spirit often sees beyond these biases. They focus on building genuine connections, often becoming ambassadors of their rich culture and, in the process, shattering misconceptions.

Building Bridges Through Optimism

The optimism of Nigerian immigrants isn't insular. It extends beyond the individual and influences the community at large:

1. Creating Supportive Communities: Nigerian immigrants often form close-knit communities in their adopted countries. These communities, buoyed by collective optimism, become hubs of mutual support, shared experiences, and collective celebrations. They serve as reminders that challenges can be surmounted when faced together.

2. Mentorship: Many successful Nigerian immigrants, driven by their optimistic belief in paying it forward, take on mentorship roles. They guide newer immigrants, offering advice, sharing resources, and providing moral support, ensuring that the journey becomes a tad easier for the next person.

Case Studies in Optimism

There are countless stories within the Nigerian immigrant community that serve as testimonies to the power of optimism. From professionals who rose through the ranks in corporate structures, artists who made a mark globally, to entrepreneurs who built successful enterprises from scratch - their journeys, though diverse, share the undercurrent of undying optimism.

The optimism ingrained in the Nigerian psyche isn't a fleeting emotion; it's a steadfast belief, a guiding philosophy. For Nigerian immigrants, this optimism acts as the wind beneath their wings, propelling them forward, even when the skies seem overcast with challenges. It reminds them that beyond the darkest clouds, the sun still shines, waiting for its moment to break through. More often than not, driven by this optimism, Nigerian immigrants not only weather the storm but also dance in the rain, celebrating the journey and the destination.

Nigerian Immigrants: Beacons of Success in Global Arenas

Nigeria is often referred to as the "Giant of Africa," not only due to its substantial population but also because of the immense talent that originates from its shores. Its emigrants, a testament to its rich reservoir of brilliance, have achieved considerable success in various parts of the world. From arts to academia, business to sports, Nigerian immigrants have consistently shone, proving their mettle and making their homeland proud. In this chapter, we celebrate the success stories of these stellar individuals.

From Naija to the World: A Success Symphony

1. Literature & Arts: The literary world has been significantly enriched by Nigerian talent. Chimamanda Ngozi Adichie, for instance, has become a global voice for feminism and African narratives. Her novels, such as "Half of a Yellow Sun" and "Americanah," have been celebrated worldwide, winning numerous awards. Similarly, Wole Soyinka, a playwright and poet, brought honor to Nigeria by becoming the first African laureate to be awarded the Nobel Prize in Literature.

2. Science & Medicine: The global scientific community has witnessed the prowess of Nigerian immigrants. One such shining star is Dr. Bennet Omalu, a Nigerian-American physician, forensic pathologist, and neuropathologist. He was the first to discover and publish findings on the brain disease Chronic Traumatic Encephalopathy (CTE) in American football players, a revelation that shook the sports world.

3. Entrepreneurship: Nigerian immigrants have showcased their entrepreneurial flair in various sectors. Igho Sanomi, founder of Taleveras, is a perfect example. His business acumen turned Taleveras into one of Africa's leading energy groups. Another commendable figure is Femi Otedola, a business magnate who has had success in Nigeria and beyond with ventures in various sectors, including energy, real estate, and finance.

4. Entertainment: The entertainment sector has seen the rise of numerous Nigerian personalities. Renowned musicians like Burna Boy and Wizkid have found immense success internationally, with their music being celebrated on global platforms like the Grammy Awards. In Hollywood, David Oyelowo, with roles in movies like "Selma," and Chiwetel Ejiofor, known for his role in "12 Years a Slave", have cemented their places as accomplished actors of Nigerian descent.

5. Public Service & Activism: Nigerian immigrants have also made significant strides in the realms of public service and activism. Ngozi Okonjo-Iweala, a Nigerian-American economist and international development expert, recently shattered ceilings by becoming the first woman and the first African to lead the World Trade Organization.

6. Sports: The world of sports boasts of exemplary figures of Nigerian descent. Hakeem Olajuwon, one of the greatest NBA players of all time, and Anthony Joshua, the unified world heavyweight boxing champion, both have Nigerian roots and have often expressed pride in their heritage.

The Underlying Factors

Several elements contribute to the significant success of Nigerian immigrants:

1. Solid Educational Foundation: Nigeria places a strong emphasis on education. The rigorous academic training many immigrants receive in Nigeria becomes a foundation upon which they build their global successes.

2. Resilience & Determination: The Nigerian spirit is renowned for its resilience. The ability to persevere, even in the face of adversity, is a hallmark of many success stories.

3. Community Support: Nigerian immigrants often enjoy robust support from their communities abroad. These networks provide guidance, mentorship, and resources that play a pivotal role in individual success.

The success stories of Nigerian immigrants underscore the nation's immense potential and the global relevance of its human capital. These tales of triumph, borne out of a blend of innate talent, hard work, resilience, and the spirit of Ubuntu (African humanism), inspire not just the Nigerian diaspora but people worldwide.

While challenges remain and the journey for many is far from easy, the remarkable accomplishments of these immigrants serve as beacons of hope and a testament to what is achievable when potential meets opportunity. As the world continues to witness the rise of Nigeria through its emigrants, one thing is clear: the Nigerian star shines brightly on the global stage.

Chapter 13: Community Support

Together We Rise - The Power of Community Support in Nigerian Culture

In many African societies, there's a saying: "It takes a village to raise a child." This proverb underscores the vital role community plays in individual upbringing and success. For Nigeria, with its rich tapestry of ethnicities and cultures, the concept of community isn't just tradition - it's a way of life. From the bustling streets of Lagos to the serene landscapes of Enugu, the essence of community weaves Nigerians together, influencing both life in the homeland and the diasporic experience.

The Essence of Community in Nigerian Culture

1. **Extended Family Systems:** At the heart of Nigerian culture lies the extended family system. It's not just about nuclear families;

cousins, uncles, aunts, grandparents, and even distant relatives play crucial roles in an individual's life. This network provides both material and emotional support, ensuring members never feel isolated, no matter the circumstance.

2. Festivals & Celebrations: Regular communal gatherings, such as weddings, naming ceremonies, and traditional festivals, are essential facets of Nigerian culture. They provide opportunities for members to connect, celebrate shared histories, and strengthen bonds.

3. Collective Responsibility: In Nigerian communities, challenges faced by one are often viewed as challenges faced by all. Whether it's raising funds for a medical emergency, contributing towards educational expenses, or aiding a family in crisis, the community stands united.

Nigerian Immigrants and the Role of Community Support Abroad

1. Forming Micro-Communities: Upon arriving in a new country, it's common for Nigerian immigrants to seek out fellow countrymen and form tight-knit communities. Cities across the world, from Houston to London, have thriving Nigerian communities that celebrate cultural festivals, enjoy Nigerian cuisine, and provide a home away from home.

2. Resource Sharing: These diasporic communities become vital resource hubs. From tips on the best Nigerian grocery stores to recommendations for professionals who understand the nuances of Nigerian traditions, these communities ensure members have access to familiar comforts.

3. Emotional & Financial Support: The challenges of settling in a new country, from homesickness to financial hurdles, can be daunting. The immigrant community often steps in to provide emotional support, financial aid, or even job referrals. It's not uncommon for established immigrants to mentor newcomers, guiding them through the initial hurdles.

4. Cultural Preservation: While integration into the host country is crucial, these communities also play a vital role in preserving Nigerian culture. Through organized events, language classes, and cultural programs, they ensure that younger generations stay connected to their roots.

Success Stories Rooted in Community

Numerous Nigerian immigrants have achieved significant success, with their community playing a pivotal role in their journey.

Academic Achievements: It's a well-known fact that many Nigerians immigrants excel in academics abroad. Behind many such success stories are community study groups, scholarship funds established by community elders, or mentorship programs that guide students.

Entrepreneurial Ventures: Many successful Nigerian-owned businesses abroad began with community support, be it through initial funding pooled by community members or the loyal patronage of the Nigerian diaspora.

Arts & Entertainment: Many Nigerian artists who have gained international acclaim, like the musician Burna Boy or author Chimamanda Ngozi Adichie, have often credited their community for its unwavering support, especially during the early days of their careers.

The strength of the Nigerian spirit is amplified when bolstered by community. Deep ingrained in Nigerian culture, this communal ethos becomes a beacon for immigrants, illuminating their paths in unfamiliar terrains. As they forge ahead, building new lives and scaling heights, the community remains their steady anchor, a reminder of their roots, and a testament to the African saying, "If you want to go fast, go alone; if you want to go far, go together." In the journey of Nigerian immigrants, they don't just go far - they soar with their community by their side.

Rising with the Tide - How Community Lifts Nigerian Immigrants to Success

The narrative of immigrant success is a global tapestry woven with threads of hard work, determination, and, often, sacrifice. But for many Nigerian immigrants, an additional, invaluable thread runs consistently through their stories: the unwavering support of their community. The proverbial African village extends beyond the shores of the continent to touch every corner of the globe where a Nigerian sets foot. This chapter delves deep into the stories of Nigerian immigrants whose achievements were not just their own but that of a collective spirit, exemplified by the community's support.

The Community's Hand in Success

Across disciplines, sectors, and continents, Nigerian immigrants have thrived. Behind the scenes, the role of their community often stands as a significant pillar:

1. Financial Aid: For many immigrants, especially those who venture into business or higher studies, initial capital or fees pose a substantial challenge. Here, the community often steps in, pooling resources or setting up funds to provide loans and grants.

2. Networking: The power of community lies not just in financial or emotional support but also in its vast network. Established community members often mentor newcomers, introduce them to industry contacts, or provide job references.

3. **Cultural Anchoring:** Integrating into a new society while retaining one's cultural identity can be a delicate balance. The community provides a space where one can be unabashedly Nigerian, seek solace in familiar traditions, and draw strength from shared experiences.

4. Skill Sharing and Training: Within many Nigerian immigrant communities, successful individuals offer workshops or training sessions to equip fellow members with needed skills, be it in IT, business management, or even arts.

Uzodinma Iweala: A Nigerian-American Writer and Medical Doctor

Uzodinma Iweala stands as a remarkable figure in the literary and medical fields, seamlessly merging his Nigerian-American heritage with his multifaceted talents. As the author of influential novels such as "Beasts of No

Nation," "Speak No Evil," and "Bêtes sans patrie: roman," and the nonfiction work "Our Kind of People: Thoughts on the HIV/AIDS Epidemic," Iweala's writings have garnered international acclaim for their insightful portrayal of the Nigerian experience. His contributions extend to prestigious publications like The New York Times, The Guardian, and Granta.

A Journey Across Continents: Early Life and Education

Iweala's story began in Okwudor, Nigeria, in 1982. His transition to the United States at the age of 13 marked the beginning of a journey that would see him excel in both medicine and literature. A graduate of Columbia University's medical program, he practiced as a doctor in New York City, showcasing his commitment to healing and empathy.

Literary Pursuits: A Blend of Fiction and Reality

Iweala's literary debut, "Beasts of No Nation," released in 2005, is a poignant and semi-autobiographical narrative of a child soldier's harrowing experiences. This work, which earned nominations for the Man Booker Prize and won the Guardian Fiction Prize, set the stage for his subsequent novels. "Speak No Evil," published in 2012, is a riveting thriller that delves into themes of race, identity, and politics in Nigeria. In 2019, "Our Kind of People: Thoughts on the HIV/AIDS Epidemic" further showcased Iweala's literary prowess, offering a deeply personal and historical perspective on HIV/AIDS in Nigeria.

The Intersection of Medicine and Writing

Iweala's medical career is as distinguished as his literary one. As a licensed physician in the United States, he has practiced in New York

City, Abuja, and Lagos, and he has contributed his expertise as a visiting faculty member at the Johns Hopkins School of Public Health.

Accolades and Contributions to Society

Iweala's work has not only earned him literary awards but also prestigious honors like the MacArthur Fellowship, the Guggenheim Fellowship, and the National Book Critics Circle Award. His election to the American Academy of Arts and Sciences attests to his broad impact.

A Legacy Beyond Borders

Uzodinma Iweala's legacy is multifaceted. As a writer, he provides a powerful voice for Nigerians and African immigrants. As a medical doctor, he embodies the ideals of service and compassion. His work is poised to leave an indelible mark on generations to come.

Additional Noteworthy Achievements

- Iweala is the son of Ngozi Okonjo-Iweala, the former Director-General of the World Trade Organization, which speaks to a family legacy of global impact.

- He co-founded Ventures Africa, a magazine dedicated to covering business, politics, culture, and innovation across the continent.

- He is also a co-founder of The Africa Center in New York City, a cultural institution that fosters understanding and appreciation of African art, culture, and education.

Uzodinma Iweala's life and work represent a unique blend of art, science, and advocacy. His achievements in writing and medicine, coupled with his dedication to cultural and social issues, make him an inspirational figure in the global community.

Chapter 14: Education Abroad

Pursuit of Excellence - Education Abroad in Nigerian Culture

In Nigeria, a nation with a rich history and diverse tapestry of cultures, education is often seen as the golden key to success. This reverence for education isn't just limited to the homeland; it transcends borders. As globalization narrows the gap between continents, the allure of education abroad has grown profoundly in Nigerian culture. This chapter delves into the intricate relationship between Nigerians and overseas education, exploring the reasons behind its importance and the transformative role it plays in the lives of many Nigerian immigrants.

The Pedestal of Overseas Education in Nigerian Culture

1. Prestige and Esteem: Historically, a degree from a foreign university, especially from Western nations, has been viewed with immense respect in Nigeria. Such a degree is often associated with a superior quality of education, enhancing the holder's prestige.

2. Broadening Horizons: Education abroad offers Nigerians an opportunity to immerse themselves in different cultures, perspectives, and ways of life. This global exposure is deemed invaluable, equipping individuals with a more holistic worldview.

3. Better Opportunities: Many Nigerians believe that overseas education opens the door to a wider array of opportunities, be it in terms of job prospects, research, or entrepreneurial ventures.

4. Legacy of the Elite: In Nigeria's post-independence era, many leaders and individuals of high societal standing were educated abroad. This legacy has created an aspirational value around foreign education.

Education Abroad: A Stepping Stone for Nigerian Immigrants

For many Nigerian immigrants, education abroad isn't just about acquiring a degree; it's a multifaceted journey that shapes their future.

1. A Foot in the Door: A foreign degree often becomes a pathway for Nigerians to settle in a new country, navigate its job market, and integrate into its society.

2. Networking: Universities abroad provide Nigerian students with a platform to establish networks with fellow Nigerians and a diverse international community. These networks often prove invaluable as they venture into their respective professions.

3. Skill Enhancement: Apart from academic knowledge, overseas education instills a range of soft skills in students, from cross-cultural communication to problem-solving in diverse teams.

4. A Launchpad for Ambitions: For many Nigerians, studying abroad serves as a stepping stone for bigger aspirations, be it launching a global startup, delving into international research, or climbing the corporate ladder in multinational companies.

Education, in Nigerian culture, is deeply revered. It symbolizes hope, ambition, and the promise of a brighter future. When this education extends beyond the nation's borders, it embodies knowledge, the spirit of exploration, and the dream of global success.

The stories of Nigerian immigrants, be they engineers in Silicon Valley, researchers in European labs, or financial experts in the skyscrapers of New York, often begin in the classrooms of foreign universities. These classrooms serve as melting pots, where the rich heritage of Nigeria merges with global insights, crafting individuals who are ambassadors of their culture and flagbearers of global excellence.

In the grand narrative of Nigerian success overseas, education abroad stands as a monumental chapter, echoing the nation's belief in the transformative power of knowledge. For many Nigerians, the journey of success, marked by challenges and triumphs, begins with a dream of education beyond their homeland's shores amidst global arenas of excellence.

Beyond Borders - The Success Tales of Nigerian Immigrants

In the annals of immigrant success stories in the United States, the narrative of Nigerian immigrants stands out. A unique blend of determination, heritage, and the enriching experience of education abroad often sets the stage for their impressive achievements. This chapter highlights the inspiring journeys of such individuals, focusing on how their foreign education became a catalyst in realizing their American dreams.

Nigerian Immigrants: An Education Beyond Classrooms

For many Nigerian immigrants, studying abroad isn't merely an academic venture. The experience encompasses:

1. Cultural Assimilation: Navigating life in a foreign land, understanding its social intricacies, and blending into its culture molds students into adaptable and globally aware individuals.

2. Broadened Perspectives: Exposure to diverse viewpoints, ideologies, and methodologies provides these students with a more rounded approach to problem-solving.

3. Networking: Universities abroad serve as nexus points for international relations. The connections formed here often lay the foundation for future collaborations and career opportunities.

4. Skill Acquisition: The holistic nature of education abroad equips students with both hard skills related to their field of study and soft skills like communication, leadership, and teamwork.

From Nigerian Campuses to American Pinnacles: Stories of Triumph

Nigerian immigrants have left an indelible mark across various sectors in the US, from technology and finance to arts and governance. Their stories often trace back to their time spent in foreign universities, where they not only amassed knowledge but also honed their character:

1. Tech Innovators: Many Nigerian immigrants who pursued tech degrees abroad now spearheads innovations in Silicon Valley, leveraging their unique blend of Nigerian ingenuity and foreign training.

2. Medical Pioneers: With medical degrees from esteemed international institutions, several Nigerian doctors and researchers are at the forefront of healthcare advancements in the US.

3. Cultural Ambassadors: Nigerian immigrants with backgrounds in arts and humanities from global institutions have enriched the American cultural scene, be it through literature, music, or cinema.

4. Policy Makers and Thought Leaders: Armed with degrees in law, economics, and public policy from world-renowned universities, many Nigerians have ventured into the spheres of governance and policy-making in the US, making impactful contributions.

Adewale Adeyemo: A Beacon of Inspiration

A shining example in this tapestry of success stories is Adewale (Wally) Adeyemo. His journey from Nigeria to becoming the first deputy national security advisor for economic policy in the Biden administration is nothing short of inspiring.

Adeyemo's pursuit of education took him from Nigeria to the University of California, Berkeley, and later to Yale Law School. These institutions didn't just impart knowledge; they shaped his worldview, enabling him to grasp global economic intricacies and interdependencies.

His foreign education was instrumental in sharpening his analytical abilities, fostering a deeper understanding of multicultural dynamics, and equipping him with a nuanced perspective on international relations.

Adeyemo's role required him to navigate complex economic policies, not just within the domestic framework of the US but in relation to global economies. The cosmopolitan exposure of his education abroad was pivotal in these endeavors.

In his reflections, Adeyemo often emphasizes the significance of his time spent at these foreign institutions. He believes that understanding different cultures and perspectives is not just an academic exercise but a life lesson. This comprehension has been instrumental in his negotiations, policy formulations, and diplomatic relations, making him a celebrated figure in economic circles and beyond.

The success stories of Nigerian immigrants in the US, illuminated by figures like Adewale

Adeyemo serves as a testament to the transformative power of education abroad. These narratives underscore the idea that education, especially when pursued across borders, becomes more than just degrees and certificates; it becomes a bridge connecting aspirations with realities. For many Nigerians in America, their foreign alma maters stand as silent yet profound pillars behind their towering achievements.

Chapter 15: The Future of Nigerian Immigrants

The Future Horizon - Nigerian Immigrants in the United States

The mosaic of America's immigrant populace has seen a dynamic and spirited addition with the influx of Nigerians, a community known for its vibrant culture, resolute spirit, and academic prowess. With an impressive trajectory of accomplishments in their past and present, the prospects of Nigerian immigrants in the United States beckon an optimistic future. This chapter delves into the probable pathways, opportunities, and contributions of this community, painting a picture of their foreseeable journey in America.

Past and Present: Setting the Stage

To understand the future, one must first appreciate the past. Historically, Nigerian immigrants have showcased:

1. Academic Excellence: Nigerians are one of the most educated immigrant groups in the US, with a significant percentage holding bachelor's degrees and beyond.

2. Economic Contributions: From technology to medicine, Nigerian immigrants have made substantial contributions to the US economy.

3. Cultural Integration: While holding onto their roots, Nigerians have embraced American culture, enriching the societal fabric with their traditions, music, and cuisine.

The Promising Path Ahead

With such a foundational legacy, the future of Nigerian immigrants in the United States appears bright and filled with potential.

1. Elevated Socio-Economic Status: Nigerian immigrants' academic and professional diligence is likely to propel them to even higher socio-economic strata, giving them a more significant influence in various sectors.

2. Increased Political Participation: As integration continues, more Nigerian Americans are expected to participate in the US political arena, possibly taking up essential roles in local and federal governance.

3. Strengthened Bilateral Ties: The Nigerian diaspora can act as a bridge, strengthening economic, cultural, and diplomatic ties between Nigeria and the US.

4. Enriched American Cultural Scene: The influence of Nigerian art, literature, music, and cinema is expected to grow, further entrenching its presence in mainstream American culture.

5. Championing Innovations: Given their penchant for innovation and entrepreneurship, it's foreseeable that Nigerian immigrants will be at the forefront of various technological, medical, and creative breakthroughs.

6. Community Cohesion and Support: As their numbers grow, Nigerian immigrant communities will likely form stronger support systems, helping new immigrants integrate and succeed.

Challenges and Resilience

While the future brims with promise, it isn't devoid of challenges. The Nigerian immigrant community will likely face:

1. Navigating Identity: Straddling between Nigerian roots and American identity might lead to internal cultural conflicts, especially among the younger generation.

2. Racial Dynamics: As with other immigrants groups, Nigerians will continue to navigate the intricate racial dynamics in the US.

3. Geopolitical Factors: The relationship between the US and Nigeria, along with global political climates, can influence the experiences of Nigerian immigrants.

However, given the community's inherent resilience, adaptability, and the wealth of their contributions, it's anticipated that they will navigate these challenges successfully, turning potential setbacks into opportunities for growth.

A Visionary Perspective: What Lies Beyond 2050?

Peering further into the horizon, beyond immediate decades, it's conceivable that Nigerian immigrants will:

1. Hold Influential Leadership Roles: From tech conglomerates to political offices, Nigerian

Americans may hold pivotal leadership roles, shaping policies and innovations.

2. Act as Global Ambassadors: With feet in both worlds, they might play an essential role in global diplomacy and business, linking continents.

3. Drive Socio-Cultural Movements: Drawing from their unique vantage point, Nigerian immigrants can drive and influence socio-cultural movements, championing inclusivity, diversity, and global unity.

The narrative of Nigerian immigrants in the United States is one of perseverance, ambition, and significant contributions. As the chapters of this story continue to unfold, the United States stands to gain immensely from the talents, insights, and spirit of this vibrant community.

Rooted in their rich heritage and equipped with the experiences of their adopted homeland, Nigerian immigrants are poised to sculpt a future marked by success, influence, and lasting impact. The tapestry of America's future, interwoven with the threads of Nigerian brilliance, promises a vista of shared prosperity and mutual growth.

Ripple Effects - Nigerian Immigrant Success and Its Broader Implications

The narrative of Nigerian immigrants in the United States is not just a tale of individual or community success; it's a potent illustration of the broader transformative potential that immigration brings. From bustling city centers to academic hallways, Nigerian immigrants have cemented their reputation as diligent,

innovative, and successful contributors to American society. As we gaze into the future, it's essential to understand how this success will reverberate, influencing other African immigrant groups and the very fabric of America.

The African Immigrant Story: A Tapestry of Diverse Journeys

1. Empowered Narratives: The triumphs of Nigerian immigrants provide a counter-narrative to often stereotypical perceptions about African nations and their citizens. As Nigerians soar in various fields, they uplift the collective image of Africa, spotlighting the continent's potential and refuting reductive notions.

2. Blueprint for Success: The pathways carved by Nigerians can serve as roadmaps for other African immigrants. Their tales of integration, education, and entrepreneurship can guide newcomers, highlighting best practices and pitfalls to avoid.

3. Strengthened Inter-Community Bonds: The successes of one African immigrant group can foster stronger bonds between different African communities in the US. This pan-African solidarity can lead to collaborative ventures, socio-cultural events, and united efforts to address common challenges.

A Changed America: Broadening Horizons and Breaking Barriers

1. Enriched Socio-Cultural Fabric: As Nigerian immigrants excel and integrate, they introduce America to their rich tapestry of traditions, stories, music, and culinary delights. This cultural exchange leads to a more diverse, inclusive, and enriched societal milieu, where Americans gain a broader perspective of the world.

2. Economic Gains: Nigerian success stories, especially in entrepreneurship, have bolstered the American economy. As these businesses grow, they create jobs and open doors for international partnerships, fostering a robust economic link between Africa and the US.

3. Education and Innovation: With a high emphasis on education, Nigerians have made significant contributions to academia and research. Their successes paved the way for further collaboration between American institutions and African counterparts, leading to a cross-pollination of ideas and innovations.

4. Political Dynamics: As Nigerians and, by extension, other African immigrants become more involved in American politics, they bring fresh perspectives to the table. Their participation ensures that policies are more globally informed and inclusive.

Implications for Other African Immigrants

1. Amplified Voices: The prominence of Nigerian immigrants can give other African communities a platform, amplifying their voices and concerns on a larger scale.

2. Shared Resources and Networks: As Nigerian immigrant networks expand, they can extend support to other African immigrants, be it in the form of community resources, job opportunities, or mentorship.

3. Inspiration: Witnessing the success of Nigerian immigrants can inspire other African communities to pursue their dreams relentlessly, fostering a spirit of mutual encouragement and shared aspirations.

A Unifying Future: A Nation Redefined

As the Nigerian immigrant success narrative unfolds, it has the potential to redefine American perceptions about Africa. Gone will be the days of viewing the continent merely as a monolithic entity rife with challenges. Instead, the focus will shift to its richness, diversity, potential, and the shared values that bind humanity across borders.

This positive shift can lead to more inclusive policies, better diplomatic relations, and a surge in socio-cultural and economic exchanges between the US and African nations. More than just numbers or economic contributors, Nigerian immigrants and their successes will stand as a testament to America's age-old belief – that it is a land of dreams, where every individual, irrespective of their origin, has the potential to redefine the nation's destiny.

The ripples created by the success of Nigerian immigrants are not confined within community boundaries; they promise to impact broader shores. As these waves touch other African communities and the American populace at large, they bring with them lessons of perseverance, the beauty of diversity, and the limitless potential that lies in collaborative growth. In the grand tapestry of America's future, the threads woven by Nigerian immigrants will undoubtedly shine bright, illuminating pathways for many more to come.

A Portrait of Teju Cole: A Nigerian American Writer and Photographer

Teju Cole stands as a pivotal figure in contemporary literature and photography, bridging diverse worlds with his Nigerian-American heritage. Renowned for his novels "Open City," "Every Day Is for the Thief," and "Known and Strange Things," as well as his photobook "Punto d'Ombra," Cole's oeuvre is celebrated for its profound intelligence, aesthetic beauty, and insightful exploration of the African immigrant experience. Additionally, his role as a contributing editor to The New

Yorker underscores his influence in the literary world.

The Intersection of Two Worlds: Cole's Early Life and Education

Born in Kalamazoo, Michigan, to Nigerian parents, Cole's life has been a rich tapestry of cultural experiences. Growing up in Nigeria and the United States, he was exposed to a myriad of perspectives that deeply influenced his artistic and intellectual pursuits. His academic journey, encompassing art history and English at Swarthmore College and Columbia University, laid the foundation for his multifaceted career.

The Emergence of a Literary Voice

Cole's literary journey began with a profound exploration of the African immigrant narrative. His debut novel, "Open City," released in 2011, delves into the complexities of a young Nigerian man's life in New York City, earning acclaim for its sensitive portrayal of the immigrant experience. This theme of identity and displacement continues in his 2014 novel, "Every Day Is for the Thief," a gripping narrative that intertwines crime and corruption in Nigeria.

2016 saw the release of "Known and Strange Things," a collection of essays that delve into a spectrum of topics including race, identity, and politics, lauded for their incisive and honest commentary. The same year, Cole's "Punto d'Ombra" brought to light his photographic prowess, capturing the nuances of Nigerian life in striking black-and-white imagery.

Accolades and Recognition

Teju Cole's contributions to literature and photography have not gone unnoticed. He is a recipient of prestigious awards such as the MacArthur Fellowship, the PEN Open Book Award, and the Windham-Campbell Literature

Prize. His membership in the American Academy of Arts and Sciences further cements his status as a significant cultural figure.

The Artistry of Teju Cole

Cole's writing is marked by a profound understanding and manipulation of language, creating evocative and vivid imagery. His astute observations of human nature allow him to present the complexities of the human condition with remarkable clarity. His focus on the African immigrant experience, dissecting themes of displacement, race, and identity, offers a fresh and necessary perspective on contemporary issues.

Similarly, his photography is a visual extension of his narrative skill. The monochromatic simplicity of his photographs reveals the everyday realities of Nigeria, offering a window into the country's soul and challenging misconceptions.

Teju Cole's Enduring Legacy

Teju Cole is more than a writer and photographer; he is a cultural ambassador, bridging continents through his art. His work does not merely narrate the African immigrant experience; it invites a global audience to reconsider their perspectives on race, identity, and politics. Cole's legacy, rooted in his unique narrative and visual storytelling, promises to influence and inspire future generations, making him a quintessential figure in the landscape of global literature and art.

References

Nigerian Americans Statistics:

1. Migration Policy Institute. (n.d.). "The Educational and Economic Success of Nigerian Immigrants in the United States."

   - URL: https://www.migrationpolicy.org/country-resource/nigeria

2. Migration Policy Institute. (n.d.). "Nigerian Americans: A Demographic Profile."

   - URL: https://www.migrationpolicy.org/sites/default/files/publications/RAD-Nigeria.pdf

3. Forbes. (n.d.). "The Rise of Nigerian Entrepreneurs in the United States."

- URL:
  https://www.benjamindada.com/
  us-companies-founded-led-
  nigerian-entrepreneurs/

4. Pew Research Center. (n.d.). "Nigerian Americans Are One of the Most Educated Groups in the United States."

   - URL:
     https://www.bet.com/article/w9h
     wjf/survey-nigerians-most-
     educated-in-the-u-s

5. Small Business Administration. (n.d.). "Nigerian Americans Are More Likely to Own Businesses Than Any Other Group."

   - URL:
     https://www.sba.gov/business-
     guide/grow-your-
     business/minority-owned-
     businesses

6. Institute for Policy Studies. (n.d.). "Nigerian Americans Are Among the Wealthiest Immigrant Groups in the United States."

- URL: https://www.aljazeera.com/features/2020/12/10/wealthy-nigerians-buying-citizenship-overseas

7. Brookings Institution. (n.d.). "Nigerian Americans Are Making Significant Contributions to the U.S. Economy."

- URL: https://www.brookings.edu/regions/africa/nigeria-2/

8. National Science Foundation. (n.d.). "Nigerian Americans Are Overrepresented in STEM Fields."

- URL: https://www.ncat.edu/news/2022/11/nsf-pfmpr-bd.php

9. National Academies of Sciences, Engineering, and Medicine. (n.d.). "Nigerian Americans Are Making a Positive Impact on American Society."

- URL: https://www.nature.com/articles/palcomms201630

10. U.S. Census Bureau. (n.d.). "The Nigerian American Community Is Growing and Thriving."

- URL: https://nationalpopulation.gov.ng/

11. American Immigration Council. (n.d.). "Nigerian Americans Are Part of the Fabric of American Society."

- URL: https://www.americanimmigrationcouncil.org/board

12. National Association of Nigerian Americans. (n.d.). "The Nigerian American Community Is a Valuable Asset to the United States."

    - URL: https://napachicago.org/

13. New America Foundation. (n.d.). "Nigerian Americans Are Helping to Shape the Future of the United States."

    - URL: https://www.quora.com/In-the-next-hundred-years-to-come-do-we-think-or-hope-that-nigeria-will-be-like-America

14. Aspen Institute. (n.d.). "Nigerian Americans Are a Source of Strength and Innovation for the United States."

- URL: https://endeavornigeria.medium.com/nigeria-ecosystem-predictions-2020-a9e453994537

15. United Nations Foundation. (n.d.). "Nigerian Americans Are Making a Difference in the World."

- URL: https://unitednigeriadiasporans.org/about.php

16. White House. (n.d.). "Nigerian Americans Are an Inspiration to Us All."

- URL: https://punchng.com/buhari-prays-successful-tenure-for-nigerian-americans-elected-in-us/

17. Library of Congress. (n.d.). "Nigerian Americans Are Part of the Great American Story."

- URL: https://www.loc.gov/item/95682553/

18. Smithsonian Institution. (n.d.). "Nigerian Americans Are a Vital Part of the American Mosaic."

- URL: https://iir.gmu.edu/immigrant-stories-dc-baltimore/nigeria

19. National Endowment for the Humanities. (n.d.). "Nigerian Americans Are Making America a More Inclusive and Welcoming Country."

- URL: https://cbcs.nigeriancbcs.com/

20. American Dream Initiative. (n.d.). "Nigerian Americans Are Building a Better Future for All."

- URL: https://www.premiumtimesng.com/news/574299-574299.html

Ngozi Okonjo-Iweala

1. Financial Times Stream: Articles and Publications related to Ngozi Okonjo-Iweala:

   - URL: https://www.ft.com/stream/83b7845a-c761-447b-971f-aa8448293da0

2. Ngozi Okonjo-Iweala's Profile on The Rockefeller Foundation:

   - URL: https://www.rockefellerfoundation.org/profile/ngozi-okonjo-iweala/

3. Ngozi Okonjo-Iweala's Profile on Forbes:

- URL:
  https://www.forbes.com/profile/ngozi-okonjo-iweala/

4. Ngozi Okonjo-Iweala's Profile on the Brookings Institution:

   - URL:
     https://www.brookings.edu/people/ngozi-okonjo-iweala-2/

5. Britannica Article: "Ngozi Okonjo-Iweala - Biography":

   - URL:
     https://www.britannica.com/biography/Ngozi-Okonjo-Iweala

6. Ngozi Okonjo-Iweala's Profile on the World Bank's Live Experts Directory:

   - URL:
     https://live.worldbank.org/en/experts/n/ngozi-okonjo-iweala

Oyekunle Ayinde "Kunle" Olukotun

1. Catalog Entry at the University of Chicago Library for Kunle Olukotun:

   - URL: https://catalog.lib.uchicago.edu/vufind/Record/8512836/Details

2. Profile on Radaris for Kunle Olukotun:

   - URL: https://radaris.com/p/Kunle/Olukotun/

3. Thread on Rattibha.com mentioning Kunle Olukotun:

   - URL: https://en.rattibha.com/thread/1696166116198908139

4. Kunle Olukotun's Profile on Kumatoo.com:

   - URL: https://www.kumatoo.com/kunle-olukotun.php

5. Kunle Olukotun's Profile on Peoplepill:

   - URL: https://peoplepill.com/i/kunle-olukotun

6. Information about Kunle Olukotun, Computer Scientist, on UrbanAreas.net:

   - URL: https://urbanareas.net/info/olukotun-kunle-computer-scientist/

7. Topic Page on Semanticscholar.org related to Kunle Olukotun:

   - URL: https://www.semanticscholar.org/topic/Kunle-Olukotun/2201244

Uzodinma Iweala

1. Uzodinma Iweala's Author Profile on Foreign Affairs:

- URL:
  https://www.foreignaffairs.com/authors/uzodinma-iweala

2. New York Times Article: "Africa Center Names Iweala and Uzodinma Co-Chairs in Harlem" (Published on April 26, 2023):

   - URL:
     https://www.nytimes.com/2023/04/26/arts/design/africa-center-iweala-uzodinma-harlem.html

3. Uzodinma Iweala's Contributor Profile on Granta:

   - URL:
     https://granta.com/contributor/uzodinma-iweala/

4. Uzodinma Iweala's Blog Posts on HarperCollins:

- URL:
  https://www.harpercollins.com/blogs/authors/uzodinma-iweala

5. Uzodinma Iweala's Author Page on Goodreads:

- URL:
  https://www.goodreads.com/author/show/27161.Uzodinma_Iweala

6. Interview with Uzodinma Iweala on "Time Sensitive" Podcast:

- URL:
  https://timesensitive.fm/episode/novelist-medical-doctor-africa-center-ceo-uzodinma-iweala/

7. Uzodinma Iweala's Profile on World Wildlife Fund (WWF) Leaders:

- URL:
  https://www.worldwildlife.org/leaders/uzodinma-iweala

Adebayo Ogunlesi

1. Article on LinkedIn: "The Man Who Owns Gatwick Airport: Nigerian Adebayo Ogunlesi" by Blessmore Dube:

   - URL: https://www.linkedin.com/pulse/man-who-owns-gatwick-aiport-nigerian-adebayo-ogunlesi-blessmore-dube

2. Adebayo Ogunlesi's Profile at the Hutchins Center for African & African American Research, Harvard University:

   - URL: https://hutchinscenter.fas.harvard.edu/people/adebayo-ogunlesi

3. Article on The Cable: "FG Describes Bayo Ogunlesi as Owner of Gatwick Airport in National Honours List":

- URL: https://www.thecable.ng/extra-fg-describes-bayo-ogunlesi-as-owner-of-gatwick-airport-in-national-honours-list

4. Article on Reporters at Large: "Adebayo Ogunlesi: The Nigerian Man Who Bought London's Second Biggest International Airport":

- URL: https://www.reportersatlarge.com/2023/04/02/adebayo-ogunlesi-the-nigerian-man-who-bought-londons-second-biggest-international-airport/

5. Adebayo Ogunlesi's Profile on Crunchbase:

- URL: https://crunchbase.com/person/adebayo-o-ogunlesi

6. Adebayo Ogunlesi's Profile on Litcaf:

   - URL: https://litcaf.com/adebayo-ogunlesi/

7. Biography of Adebayo Ogunlesi on Reference for Business:

   - URL: https://www.referenceforbusiness.com/biography/M-R/Ogunlesi-Adebayo-1953.html

8. Article on The Habari Network: "Adebayo Ogunlesi: The Man Who Bought Britain's Gatwick Airport":

   - URL: https://www.thehabarinetwork.com/adebayo-ogunlesi-the-man-who-bought-britains-gatwick-airport

9. Adebayo Ogunlesi's Speaker Profile at Stanford Law School:

- URL:
  https://conferences.law.stanford.edu/blog/speakers/adebayo-o-ogunlesi/

10. Adebayo Ogunlesi's Profile on Global Infrastructure Partners (GIP):

- URL: https://www.global-infra.com/our-team/group/partners/

11. Adebayo Ogunlesi's Board Member Profile on Kosmos Energy:

- URL:
  https://investors.kosmosenergy.com/board-member/adebayo-ogunlesi

John Dabiri

1. John O. Dabiri's Profile on Papers with Code:

- URL: https://paperswithcode.com/author/john-o-dabiri-1

2. John Dabiri's Profile on Science Friday:

   - URL: https://www.sciencefriday.com/person/john-dabiri/

3. Member Spotlight on John Dabiri on AAAS (American Association for the Advancement of Science) website:

   - URL: https://www.aaas.org/membership/member-spotlight/john-dabiri-next-frontier-deep-ocean-science-remote-controlled

4. John Dabiri's Profile on Stanford University's FPC Group website:

   - URL: http://web.stanford.edu/group/f

pc/cgi-
bin/fpcwiki/People/JohnDabiri

5. John O. Dabiri's Scientific Contributions on ResearchGate:

   - URL:
     https://www.researchgate.net/scientific-contributions/John-O-Dabiri-55331442

6. Announcement of John O. Dabiri as Centennial Chair Professor at Auburn University:

   - URL:
     https://ocm.auburn.edu/newsroom/campus_notices/2023/02/081129-dabiri-centennial-chair-professor.php

7. Article on Quanta Magazine: "What Can Jellyfish Teach Us About Fluid

Dynamics?" (Published on June 28, 2023):

- URL:
  https://www.quantamagazine.org/what-can-jellyfish-teach-us-about-fluid-dynamics-20230628/

8. Document from the University of South Florida: "John Dabiri - Virtual STEM Laboratory":

- URL:
  https://www.usf.edu/education/faculty/rosengrant-virtual-stem-laboratory/documents/john-dabiri.docx

9. Article on the Science in the News (SITN) website: "John Dabiri: The Oceanic Adventures of a Bioengineer":

- URL:
  https://sitn.hms.harvard.edu/joh

n-dabiri-the-oceanic-adventures-of-a-bioengineer/

10. John O. Dabiri's Profile on the White House's President's Council of Advisors on Science and Technology (PCAST):

- URL: https://www.whitehouse.gov/pcast/members/john-o-dabiri/

11. John Dabiri's Profile on NVIDIA's Board of Directors:

- URL: https://www.nvidia.com/en-us/about-nvidia/board-of-directors/john-dabiri/

12. John Dabiri's Profile at the California Institute of Technology (Caltech) - Mechanical and Civil Engineering Department:

- URL:
  https://mce.caltech.edu/people/jodabiri

13. John Dabiri's Profile at the California Institute of Technology (Caltech) - Engineering and Applied Science Department:

- URL:
  https://www.eas.caltech.edu/people/jodabiri

Ndidi Nwuneli

1. Ndidi Okonkwo Nwuneli's Profile on the African Leadership Institute:

   - URL: https://alinstitute.org/tutu-fellows/associates/ndidi-okonkwo-nwuneli

2. Ndidi Nwuneli's Profile at the University of Cape Town Graduate School of Business:

- URL:
  https://www.gsb.uct.ac.za/profile/1166/ndidi-nwuneli

3. Ndidi Nwuneli's Speaker Profile on TED:

   - URL:
     https://www.ted.com/speakers/ndidi_nwuneli

4. Ndidi Okonkwo Nwuneli's Speaker Profile on CIFOR-ICRAF:

   - URL: https://www.cifor-icraf.org/speaker/ndidi-okonkwo-nwuneli/

5. Ndidi Okonkwo Nwuneli's Author Profile on World Economic Forum Agenda:

   - URL:
     https://www.weforum.org/agenda/authors/ndidi-okonkwo-nwuneli/

6. Ndidi Okonkwo Nwuneli's Profile on 100 Women:

   - URL:
     https://100women.avancemedia.org/ndidiokonkwonwuneli/

7. Ndidi Nwuneli's Profile on the Global Alliance for Improved Nutrition (GAIN):

   - URL:
     https://www.gainhealth.org/ndidi-nwuneli

8. Ndidi Okonkwo Nwuneli's Profile at McGill University Max Bell School of Public Policy:

   - URL:
     https://www.mcgill.ca/maxbellschool/our-people/past-faculty/ndidi-okonkwo-nwuneli

9. Ndidi Okonkwo Nwuneli's Profile at the Center for Strategic and International Studies (CSIS):

- URL: https://www.csis.org/people/ndidi-okonkwo-nwuneli

10. Ndidi Okonkwo Nwuneli's Profile on The Rockefeller Foundation Website:

- URL: https://www.rockefellerfoundation.org/profile/ndidi-okonkwo-nwuneli/

11. Ndidi Okonkwo Nwuneli's Profile on Sahel Consulting:

- URL: https://sahelconsult.com/member/ndidi-okonkwo-nwuneli-mfr/

David Adedeji Adeleke

1. Article on Platinum Times: "Life Story of David Adedeji Adeleke (Davido)":

    - URL: https://platinumtimes.ng/life-story-of-david-adedeji-adeleke-davido/

2. David Adedeji Adeleke's Artist Profile on Gaana:

    - URL: https://gaana.com/artist/david-adedeji-adeleke

3. Biography of David Adedeji Adeleke on Partyflock:

    - URL: https://partyflock.nl/artist/9762 1/biography

4. David Adedeji Adeleke's LinkedIn Profile:

- URL:
  https://www.linkedin.com/in/david-adedeji-adeleke-830237238

5. Article on Valparaiso University: "David Adedeji Adeleke Jr - Biography, Age, and Mother":

   - URL: https://my-test.valpo.edu/en/latestnews/david-adedeji-adeleke-jr-biography-age-and-mother/

6. Grammy.com Article: "Davido: Elevating Nigerian Culture with New Music and What He'll Teach His Son about Being Black":

   - URL:
     https://www.grammy.com/news/davido-elevating-nigerian-culture-new-music-what-hell-teach-his-son-about-being-black

7. Article on MIPAD (Most Influential People of African Descent) Blog: "Meet David Adedeji Adeleke, AKA Davido":

   - URL: https://blog.mipad.org/meet-david-adedeji-adeleke-aka-davido/

8. David Adedeji Adeleke's Wikidata Entry:

   - URL: https://www.wikidata.org/wiki/Q16234484

9. Official Website of Davido:

   - URL: https://www.iamdavido.com/

Uzodinma Iweala

1. New York Times Article: "Africa Center Names Iweala and Uzodinma Co-Chairs in Harlem" (Published on April 26, 2023):

- URL:
  https://www.nytimes.com/2023/04/26/arts/design/africa-center-iweala-uzodinma-harlem.html

2. Author Profile of Uzodinma Iweala on AALBC (African American Literature Book Club):

   - URL:
     https://aalbc.com/authors/author.php?author_name=Uzodinma+Iweala

3. Uzodinma Iweala's Blog Posts on HarperCollins:

   - URL:
     https://www.harpercollins.com/blogs/authors/uzodinma-iweala

4. Interview with Uzodinma Iweala on "Time Sensitive" Podcast:

- URL:
  https://timesensitive.fm/episode/
  novelist-medical-doctor-africa-
  center-ceo-uzodinma-iweala/

5. Uzodinma Iweala's Author Page on Goodreads:

   - URL:
     https://www.goodreads.com/auth
     or/show/27161.Uzodinma_Iweala

6. Uzodinma Iweala's Profile on World Wildlife Fund (WWF) Leaders:

   - URL:
     https://www.worldwildlife.org/lea
     ders/uzodinma-iweala

7. Uzodinma Iweala's Profile at Radcliffe Institute for Advanced Study at Harvard University:

- URL:
  https://www.radcliffe.harvard.edu/people/uzodinma-iweala

8. Uzodinma Iweala's LinkedIn Profile:

- URL:
  https://www.linkedin.com/in/uzodinma-iweala-58900852

Adewale Adeyemo

1. Wally Adeyemo's Official Profile on the U.S. Department of the Treasury Website:

   - URL:
     https://home.treasury.gov/about/general-information/officials/Wally-Adeyemo

2. Adewale Adeyemo's Profile on the Empower Omaha Website:

- URL:
  https://empoweromaha.com/adewale-adeyemo/

3. Article on The Cable: "U.S. Not in Nigeria to Counter Foreign Governments - Wale Adeyemo Addresses Concerns over China's Influence":

   - URL:
     https://www.thecable.ng/us-not-in-nigeria-to-counter-foreign-governments-wale-adeyemo-addresses-concerns-over-chinas-influence

4. Article on The Cable: "Adeyemo: US Deputy Treasury Secretary to Strengthen Bilateral Ties During Nigeria Visit":

   - URL:
     https://www.thecable.ng/adeyemo-us-deputy-treasury-secretary-

to-strengthen-bilateral-ties-
during-nigeria-visit

5. Document on GovInfo.gov: "Daily
   Compilation of Presidential Documents -
   December 2015":

   - URL:
     https://www.govinfo.gov/app/det
     ails/DCPD-201500889

Teju Cole

1. Teju Cole's Official Website:

   - URL: https://www.tejucole.com/

2. Teju Cole's About Page:

   - URL:
     https://www.tejucole.com/about-
     2/

3. Teju Cole's New York Times Author Page:

- URL: https://www.nytimes.com/by/teju-cole

4. Teju Cole's Book Review in The Guardian (2023):

   - URL: https://www.theguardian.com/books/2023/oct/20/tremor-by-teju-cole-review-art-history-and-violence

5. Teju Cole's Fiction in The New Yorker (December 4, 2023):

   - URL: https://www.newyorker.com/magazine/2023/12/04/incoming-fiction-teju-cole

6. Teju Cole's Profile at Harvard University:

- URL: https://english.fas.harvard.edu/people/teju-cole

7. Book Review of "Tremor" by Teju Cole on Vulture:

- URL: https://www.vulture.com/article/teju-cole-tremor-book-review.html

8. Teju Cole's Work Mentioned in the Financial Times:

- URL: https://www.ft.com/content/42521345-b105-42ad-a7f0-2c55bd756b1b

9. Teju Cole's Work Mentioned in The Nation:

- URL: https://www.thenation.com/article/culture/teju-cole-tremor/

10.   Teju Cole's Work Mentioned in the London Review of Books:

- URL: https://www.lrb.co.uk/the-paper/v45/n21/emily-witt/multinational-soap

11.   Teju Cole's Photography Featured on LensCulture:

- URL: https://www.lensculture.com/articles/teju-cole-another-way-of-telling-teju-cole-s-blind-spot

12.   Teju Cole's New Novel Mentioned in the Los Angeles Times (October 17, 2023):

- URL: https://www.latimes.com/entertainment-arts/books/story/2023-10-17/how-teju-coles-new-novel-

<u>literally-reframes-the-black-experience</u>